Boston Common

Eleanor Burns

To freedom,

precious and worth

fighting for!

First printing March, 2002

Published by Quilt in a Day®, Inc.
1955 Diamond St, San Marcos, CA 92069

©2002 by Eleanor A. Burns Family Trust

ISBN 1-891776-09-6

Art Director Merritt Voigtlander

Table of Contents

Introduction

The Boston Common quilt is laid out similar to the city of Boston, where freedom began! The Boston Common is the oldest public park in the world, dating from 1634. It was originally pasture land belonging to William Blackstone, the first settler in the Boston area. In 1830, after almost 200 years of being reserved pasture land, it was illegal to allow cows to graze on the Common.

Today the Common is the heart of Boston, hosting dozens of special events ranging from concerts to political rallies. It's a crossroads with paths leading in all directions. The Boston Common quilt also begins with the common ground in the middle, surrounded by a wide band to contain it, and pathways of strips leading off in all directions.

In December of 2001, my youngest son Orion, and good friend and assistant, Sue Bouchard, followed these crossroads to freedom. In one direction, we visited the Public Gardens with the statue of George Washington, and the famous Duck family that grew up there. Since it was winter, we missed the graceful swan boats that graciously tour visitors around the lake.

Eleanor Burns

In another direction, a 2½ mile Freedom Trail lead us past the Park Street Church where the hymn "America" was first sung, and the Granary Burying Ground, where patriots, victims of the Boston Massacre, and families of settlers are buried. We marveled at Benjamin Franklin, proudly overlooking the site of the oldest public school in America, established by Puritan settlers in 1635. We visited the Old South Meeting House, where patriots gathered to challenge British rule, and launched the Boston Tea Party in 1773. We followed the brick Freedom trail, as the strips in the quilt! Heroes Paul Revere, John Adams, Frederick Douglass and Lucy Stone among others, walked the trail too.

For a day's jaunt, we drove to Old Sturbridge Village, where we stepped back into America's past! We explored early New England in the company of farmers, craftsmen, and colorful characters. In the Country Store, I enjoyed coordinating fabrics for my quilt that are adaptations of textiles found in the clothing and quilt collections of Old Sturbridge Village. The fabric line is called "Pockets & Housewives" after the cloth bag carried by busy 19th century housewives to keep their sewing supplies handy.

When I finally carved out time to make my queen size "Freedom Quilt," I timed myself as I sewed. Fifteen hours and seven bobbins later, the top was together! Every seam locked together and matches are perfect! My cousin, Carol Selepec, did the machine quilting in true colonial style.

May you too enjoy the freedom as you ride through this easy strip piecing!

Selecting Fabric

Nine fabrics are needed for the Boston Common quilt.

Select two different color families.
From each color family, select four fabrics in values ranging from very dark to very light.

Values should move gracefully from one fabric to the next. So fabrics tie together, at least one fabric should include colors from the other family. Include variety in the scales of prints, as large scale, medium scale, small scale, and monochromatic.

Select a background in monochromatic that transitions one color family to the next.

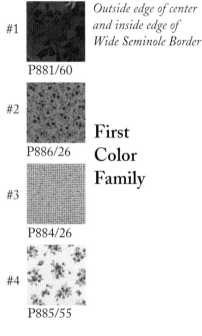

#1 *Outside edge of center and inside edge of Wide Seminole Border*

P881/60

#2

P886/26

First Color Family

#3

P884/26

#4

P885/55

#5 **Background**

#241

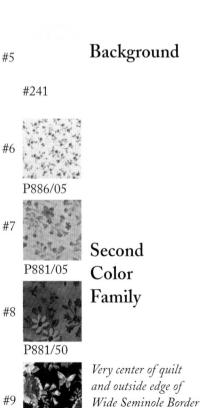

#6

P886/05

#7

P881/05

Second Color Family

#8

P881/50

#9 *Very center of quilt and outside edge of Wide Seminole Border*

P880/50

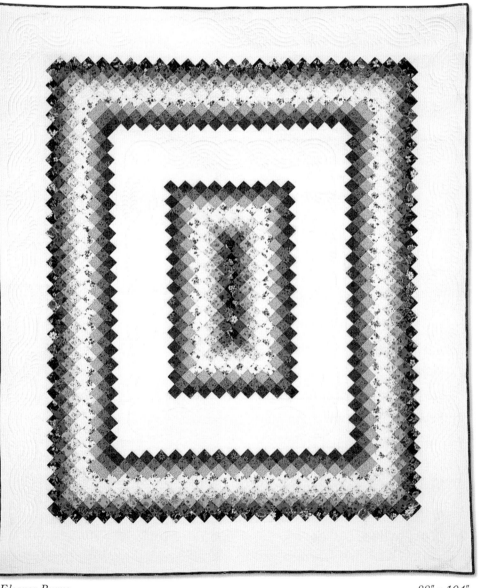

Eleanor Burns   88" x 104"

Numbers refer to fabrics in Rainbow Florals line designed by Eleanor Burns for Benartex, Inc.

The quilt photographed on the left was finished with one 8" border from Background fabric, giving plenty of space for beautiful feather quilting.

#241

P881/78

P886/50

The quilt photographed on the right was finished with a 2" border, and 6" wide floral stripe to compliment the two color families.

Outside edge of center and inside edge of Wide Seminole Border

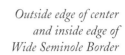

#1

P880/12

First Color Family

 #2

P881/40

 #3

P886/50

 #4

P884/05

Background

 #5

P881/01

 #6

P884/01

Second Color Family

 #7

P886/27

 #8

P886/25

Very center of quilt and outside edge of Wide Seminole Border

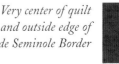 #9

P881/78

Eleanor Burns

88" x 104"

Yardage Charts
Crib Quilt

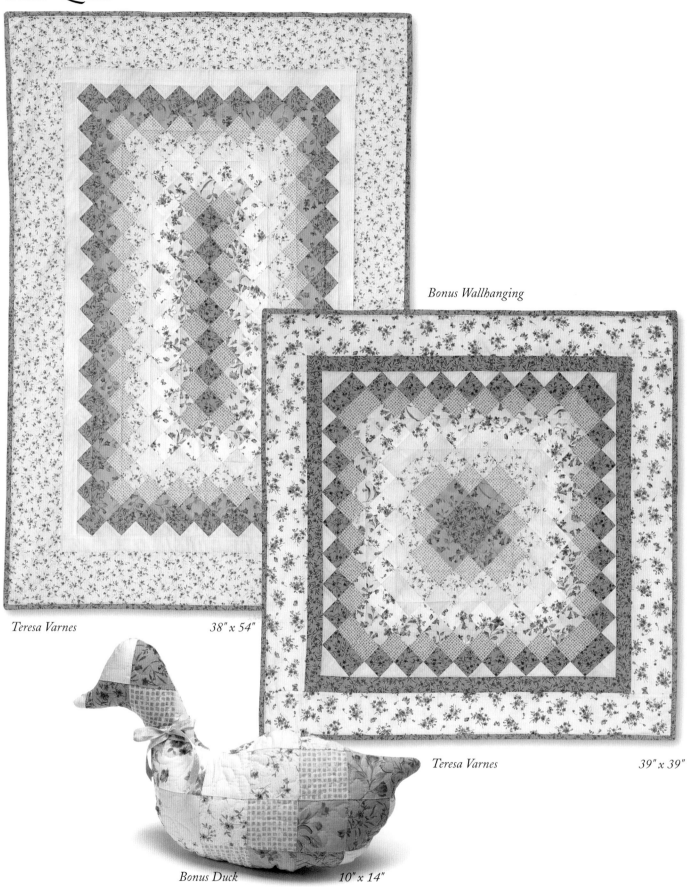

Teresa Varnes 38" x 54"

Bonus Wallhanging

Teresa Varnes 39" x 39"

Bonus Duck 10" x 14"

Perfect companions to the Crib quilt are the Bonus Wallhanging (page 91) and charming stuffed Duck (page 92) made from left-over strips. Ducks have been associated with the Boston Common since 1941, when *Make Room for Ducklings* was written by Robert McCloskey. This childhood story tells about a family of ducks that made their home in the pond at the Boston Public Garden.

First Color Family

#1 Very Dark (4) 2½" strips	⅓ yd	
P886/50		
#2 Medium Dark (4) 2½" strips	⅓ yd	
P881/05		
#3 Medium (4) 2½" strips	⅓ yd	
P884/05		
#4 Medium Light (4) 2½" strips	⅓ yd	
P886/05		

Second Color Family

#6 Medium Light (4) 2½" strips	⅓ yd	
P885/55		
#7 Medium (4) 2½" strips	⅓ yd	
P881/26		
#8 Medium Dark (4) 2½" strips	⅓ yd	
P884/26		
#9 Very Dark (4) 2½" strips	⅓ yd	
P886/60		

Background

#5 Monochromatic   1¼ yd
(4) 2½" strips
(7) 2¾" strips
(4) 2" First Border strips

P883/31

Additional Purchases

Second Border   1 yd
(5) 5½" strips

P886/05

Binding   ⅝ yd
(5) 3" strips

P886/50

Backing   1⅝ yds

Batting   45" x 60"

Lap Quilt

Eleanor Burns   54" x 70"

Bonus Pillow   28" x 28"

The Lap quilt is perfect for snuggling! To complete the ensemble, left-over strips can be turned into an oversized Bonus Pillow or Bonus Wallhanging. First Color Family requires more fabric because it is repeated in the narrow Seminole Border.

First Color Family

P881/50

#1 Very Dark ⅞ yd
(10) 2½" strips

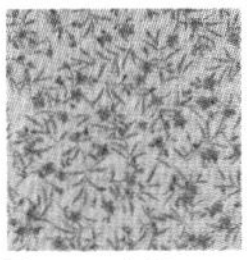
P886/50

#2 Medium Dark ⅞ yd
(10) 2½" strips

P884/05

#3 Medium ⅞ yd
(10) 2½" strips

P886/05

#4 Medium Light ⅞ yd
(10) 2½" strips

Second Color Family

P885/01

#6 Medium Light ⅓ yd
(4) 2½" strips

P886/01

#7 Medium ⅓ yd
(4) 2½" strips

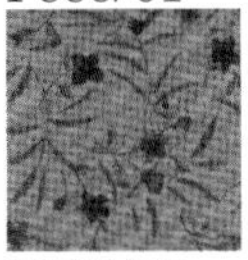
P886/27

#8 Medium Dark ⅓ yd
(4) 2½" strips

P886/25

#9 Very Dark ⅓ yd
(4) 2½" strips

Background

P881/31

#5 Monochromatic 3 yds
(4) 2½" strips
(20) 2¾" strips
(4) Inside Border strips
(cut later)

Additional Purchases

P881/31

Binding ⅝ yd
(6) 3" strips

Backing 3½ yds

Batting 60" x 76"

Twin Quilt

Teresa Varnes   *66" x 88"*

This Twin Quilt has the nostalgic charm of by-gone days in 1930's reproduction fabrics with flowers appliqued in the Inner Border. Rather than selecting two color families, a scrappy looking approach was taken. Regardless of your choice of fabric, and to applique or not, the Center for the Twin is unique because it has nine squares instead of the usual seven.

First Color Family

	#1 Very Dark (9) 2½" strips	¾ yd
	#2 Medium Dark (9) 2½" strips	¾ yd
	#3 Medium (9) 2½" strips	¾ yd
	#4 Medium Light (9) 2½" strips	¾ yd

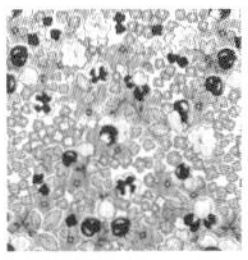

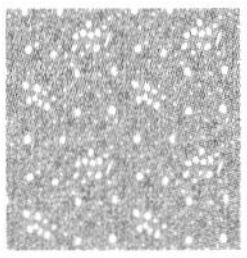

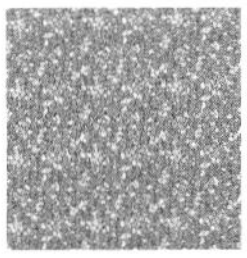

Second Color Family

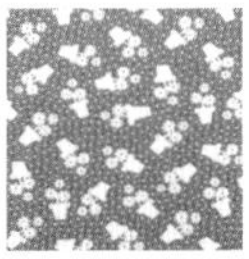

	#6 Medium Light (9) 2½" strips	¾ yd
	#7 Medium (9) 2½" strips	¾ yd
	#8 Medium Dark (9) 2½" strips	¾ yd
	#9 Very Dark (8) 2½" strips	¾ yd

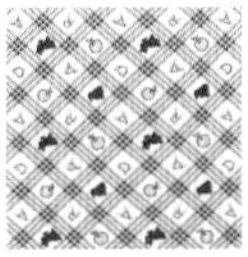

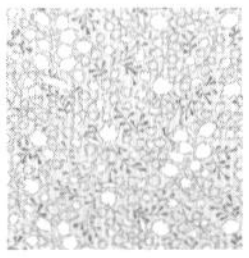

Background

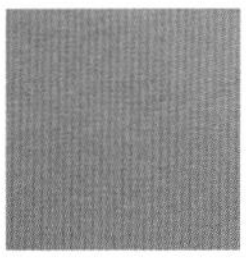

	#5 Monochromatic (9) 2½" strips (18) 2¾" strips (5) Inside Border strips (cut later)	3½ yds

Additional Purchases

	Optional Border (8) 6½" strips	1⅝ yds	Backing	4 yds
			Batting	70" x 86"
	Binding (8) 3" strips	¾ yd		

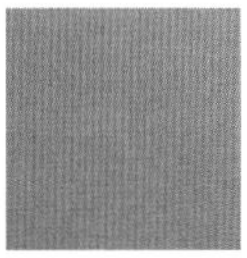

Queen Quilt

Eleanor Burns

88" x 104"

This size Boston Common is a perfect fit for the queen mattress! The Inner Border frames the edges, and the Wide Seminole Border drapes over the sides. The border choice shown is a wide 8½" border, which gives spacious room for cable and feather quilting. Since mattress depths vary, make sure you have added enough borders before machine quilting.

First Color Family

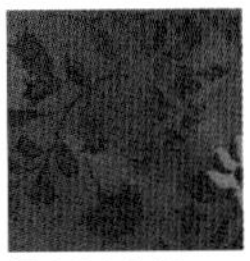
P881/60

#1 Very Dark ⅔ yd
(8) 2½" strips

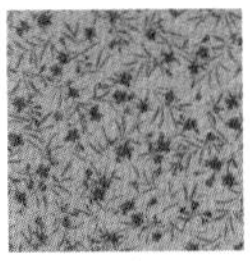
P886/26

#2 Medium Dark ⅔ yd
(8) 2½" strips

P884/26

#3 Medium ⅔ yd
(8) 2½" strips

P885/33

#4 Medium Light ⅔ yd
(8) 2½" strips

Second Color Family

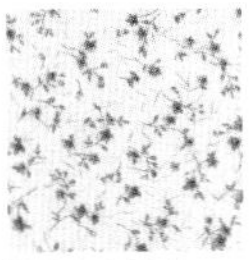
P886/05

#6 Medium Light ⅔ yd
(8) 2½" strips

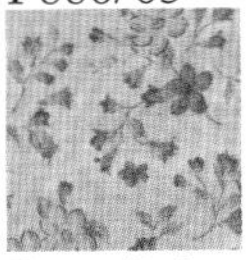
P881/05

#7 Medium ⅔ yd
(8) 2½" strips

P881/50

#8 Medium Dark ⅔ yd
(8) 2½" strips

P880/50

#9 Very Dark ⅔ yd
(8) 2½" strips

Background

#241

#5 Monochromatic 3½ yds
(8) 2½" strips
(16) 2¾" strips
(5) Inside Border strips
(cut later)

Additional Purchases

#241

One Wide Border 2¼ yds
(9) 8½" strips

or

#241

First Border ⅔ yd
(8) 2½" strips

P881/60

Second Border 1⅔ yds
(9) 6½" strips

Binding 1 yd
(10) 3" strips

Backing 8 yds

Batting 96" x 112"

King Quilt

The king size Boston Common is an extra long extravaganza! Depending on your mattress size and depth, you may want to put the Narrow Seminole Border on only three sides. Yardage for the Optional Border is for only three sides. Check your top against your mattress while under construction. First Color Family requires more strips because it is used in the Narrow Seminole Border.

First Color Family

#1 Very Dark (18) 2½" strips	1½ yds	
P880/40		
#2 Medium Dark (18) 2½" strips	1½ yds	
P881/49		
#3 Medium (18) 2½" strips	1½ yds	
P886/49		
#4 Medium Light (18) 2½" strips	1½ yds	
P885/40		

Second Color Family

#6 Medium Light (8) 2½" strips	⅔ yd	
P884/01		
#7 Medium (8) 2½" strips	⅔ yd	
P886/27		
#8 Medium Dark (8) 2½" strips	⅔ yd	
P886/25		
#9 Very Dark (8) 2½" strips	⅔ yd	
P881/78		

Background

P881/07

#5 Monochromatic   6½ yds
(8) 2½" strips
(36) 2¾" strips
(5) Inside Border strips
   (cut later)
(8) Second Inside Border strips
   (cut Later)

Additional Purchases

P881/07

Optional Border   1¼ yds
For three sides only
(8) 4½" strips

Binding   1 yd
(11) 3" strips

P881/78

Backing   9 yds

Batting   104" x 120"

Paste-Up Sheet

Make a photocopy of this page, and keep it close to your sewing and pressing for constant reference.
The purple and blue match the illustrations and the photograph of the quilt on page 14.
Cut ½" x 1" swatches from your fabric and paste in place with a glue stick.

First Color Family
Purple in illustrations

#1 Very Dark
*Outside edge of Center
Inside edge of
Seminole Border*

#2 Medium Dark

#3 Medium

#4 Medium Light

Second Color Family
Blue in illustrations

#6 Medium Light

#7 Medium

#8 Medium Dark

#9 Very Dark
*Center
Outside edge of Seminole Border*

Background

#5 Monochromatic

#5

#1

#2

#3

#4

#5

#6

#7

#8

#9

#5

Cut ¾" swatches
from your fabric
and paste in place
with a glue stick.

Supplies

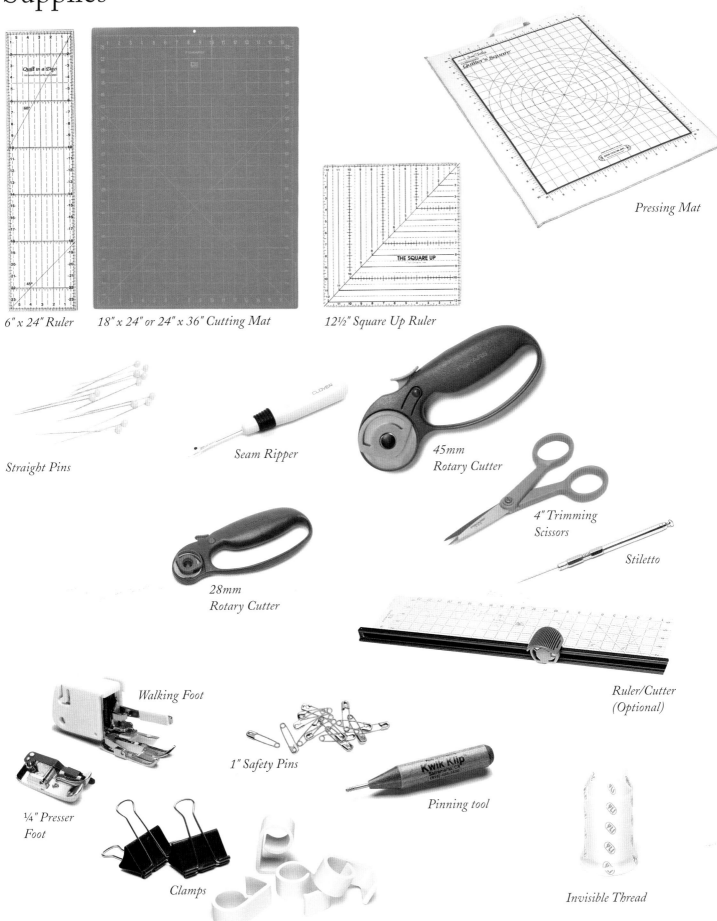

6" x 24" Ruler

18" x 24" or 24" x 36" Cutting Mat

12½" Square Up Ruler

Pressing Mat

Straight Pins

Seam Ripper

45mm Rotary Cutter

4" Trimming Scissors

Stiletto

28mm Rotary Cutter

Ruler/Cutter (Optional)

Walking Foot

1" Safety Pins

Pinning tool

¼" Presser Foot

Clamps

Invisible Thread

Quilt Parts

Each size quilt is made up of different components. They are listed in order of construction.

Twin Parts
- Center
- Center End (2)
- Wide Seminole Corner (4)
- Wide Seminole Border (4)
- Inside Border

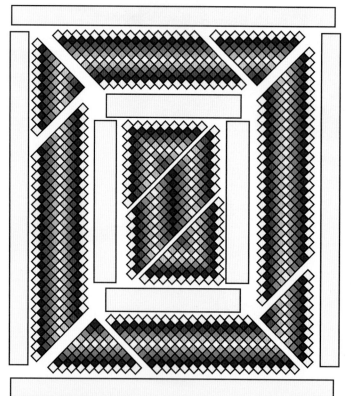

Queen Parts
- Center
- Center End (2)
- Wide Seminole Corner (4)
- Wide Seminole Border (4)
- Inside Border
- Outside Border

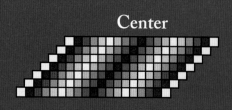

Center

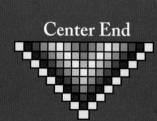

Center End

Wide Seminole Corner

Lap Parts

- Center
- Center End (2)
- Narrow Seminole Corner (4)
- Narrow Seminole Border (4)
- Inside Border

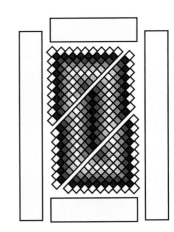

Crib Parts

- Center
- Center End (2)
- Outside Border

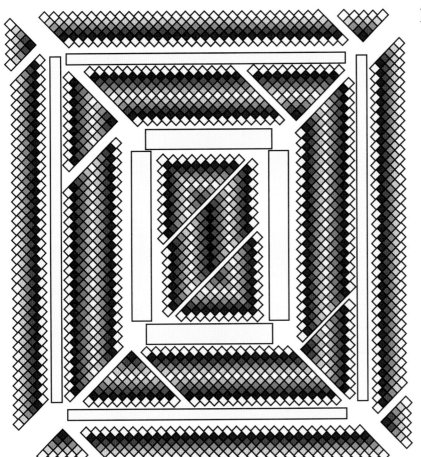

King Parts

- Center
- Center End (2)
- Wide Seminole Corner (4)
- Wide Seminole Border (4)
- Inside Border
- Narrow Seminole Corner (4)
- Narrow Seminole Border (4)
- Second Inside Border

Wide Seminole Border　　**Inside Border**　　**Narrow Seminole Corner**　　**Narrow Seminole Border**

Cutting Strips

1. Press the fabric and fold in half, lining up the straight of the grain.

2. Place the fabric on the gridded mat with the folded edge along a horizontal line. Straighten the left edge on a vertical line.

3. Place the 2½" line of the ruler along the straightened edge of the fabric.

4. Spread your fingers and place four on top of the ruler with the little finger on the mat to keep the ruler firmly in place.

5. Take the rotary cutter in your free hand and open the blade. Starting below the fabric, begin cutting away from you, applying pressure on the ruler and the cutter. Keep the blade next to the ruler's edge.

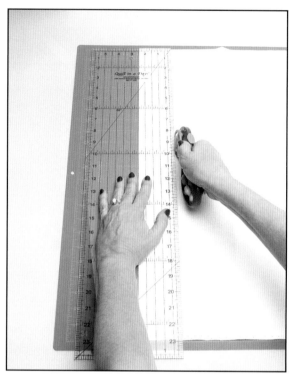

If you are right-handed the fabric should trail off to the right. The blade can be switched for left or right handed cutters.

6. **Fabrics #1 to #9 are cut 2½" wide.** For accuracy, place an adhesive strip along the 2½" line on your ruler. Open the first strip and look at the fold to see if it is straight. If it has a crook that looks like an elbow, the fabric may not be folded on the straight of the grain. If this happens, repeat the preceding steps.

7. **Fabric #5 strips are cut 2½" and 2¾" wide.** Stack in separate stacks as you cut.

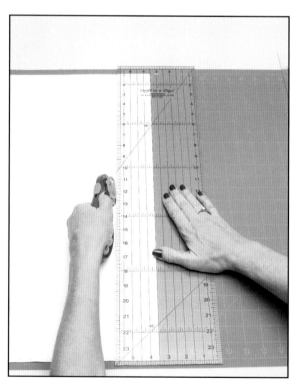

If you are left-handed the fabric should trail off to the left.

Cutting Strips in Half

All strips are cut in half with the exception of the Twin.

Twin only:
1. Count out two 2¾" strips of #5 and two 2½" strips each of Fabrics #1 to #8, and one 2½" strip of #9. Cut these strips 30" long. (See page 24). Remaining strips are cut in half on fold.

Crib, Lap, Queen and King:
2. **Cut 2¾" strips of #5 in half.** Mark with pins to designate that this strip is ¼" wider than the other strips. Keep these separate by tying together in a bundle with a scrap strip of fabric.

3. **Cut 2½" strips of the nine fabrics** by folding in half lengthwise and trimming ⅛" off the folded edge. Turn right side up. Stack each color with cut edge at top, and selvage at bottom.

4. Borders are cut at different widths. Check your particular yardage chart for measurements. Suggested widths to cut the border strips are given, but can be changed as long as you get the size quilt you desire.

The ruler/cutter combination tool is handy for cutting accurate strips. The cutter is attached to the ruler, and does not stray from ruler's edge.

Twin only: Cut approximately 30" in length.

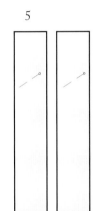

5

All other sizes: Cut approximately 20" in length.

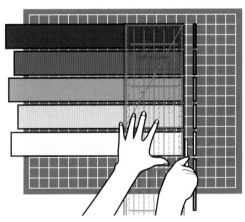

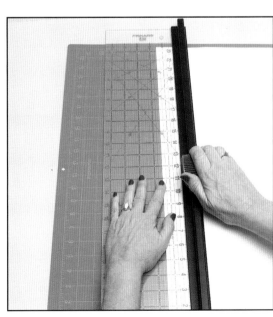

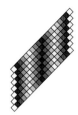

Making Center Section

Strips match photograph of Queen size quilt, page 14.

1. Arrange one strip of each in the following order. Place the 2¾" strips of #5 on outside edges. **Place cut edges at top, and selvage edges at the bottom.**

LENGTH OF STRIPS	
Crib	half strip
Lap	half strip
Twin	three fourths strip
Queen	half strip
King	half strip

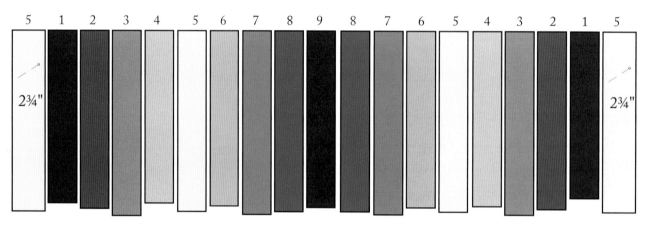

There are 19 half strips in a row with #9 strip used only once. The exception is the Twin with longer strips.

2. Divide into pairs. Starting on the left, flip #1 right sides together to #5. Flip #3 right sides together to #2.

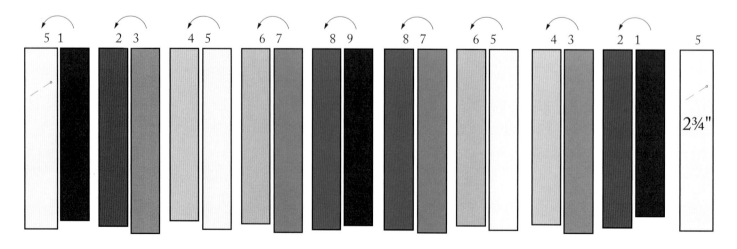

3. Continue to flip strip on right to strip on left in each pair. #5 on right is single 2¾" strip.

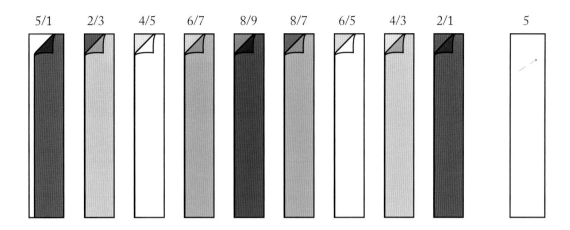

5/1 2/3 4/5 6/7 8/9 8/7 6/5 4/3 2/1 5

Sewing Strips Together

1. Pick up first pair.

2. Sew with accurate and consistent ¼" seam and 18 stitches per inch, or 1.8 on computerized machines. Continue to assembly-line sew strips together into pairs.

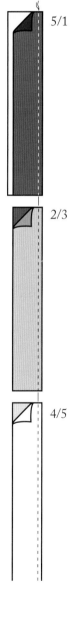

5/1

2/3

4/5

3. Clip apart beginning with last pair, and stack with first pair #5/1, ending on top.

Top pair should be #5/1.

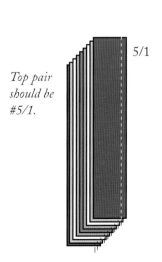

5/1

Pressing Strips

1. Use a pressing mat with grid lines and a steam iron.

2. Place first pair #5/1 on mat with #1 stitching across the top. Line up strip with lines on grid. **Cut edge is on left, and selvage is on right.**

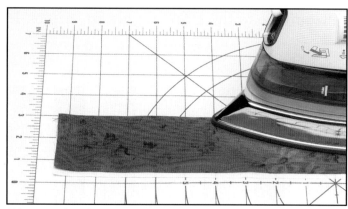

Line up strip with grid with #1 on top, and set seam.

3. Set seam of first pair with #1 on top.

4. Open, and press toward seam.

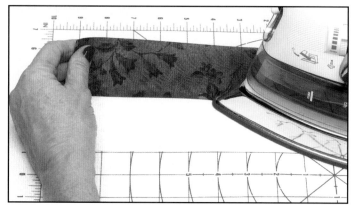

Open, and press toward seam.

5. Set seam of second pair with #3 on top.

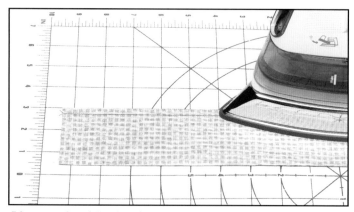

Line up strip with grid with #3 on top, and set seam.

6. Open, and press toward seam.

7. Continue to set seams and press pairs open as they were sewn.

8. **Stack in order as they are pressed.**

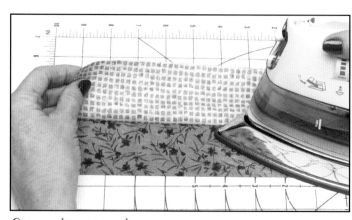

Open, and press toward seam.

Sewing Pairs Together

1. Arrange pairs in order. Starting on the left, flip #2/3 right sides together to #5/1.

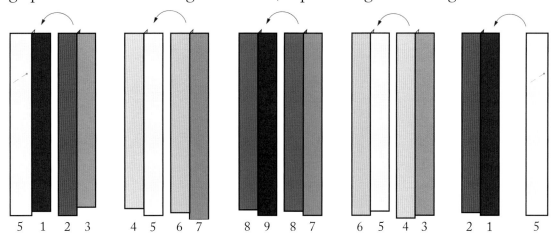

| 5 | 1 | 2 | 3 | | 4 | 5 | 6 | 7 | | 8 | 9 | 8 | 7 | | 6 | 5 | 4 | 3 | | 2 | 1 | | 5 |

2. Continue to flip all pairs right sides together.

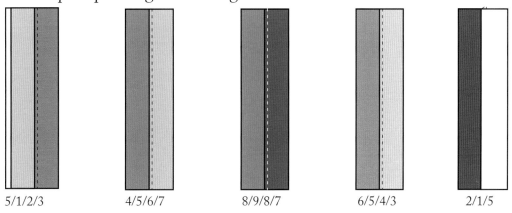

| 5/1/2/3 | 4/5/6/7 | 8/9/8/7 | 6/5/4/3 | 2/1/5 |

3. Assembly-line sew all pairs.

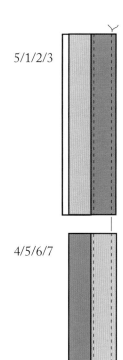

5/1/2/3

4. Clip apart starting at bottom and stack with first pair ending on top.

4/5/6/7

Pressing Strips

1. Set just sewn seam of first four with #2/3 on top.

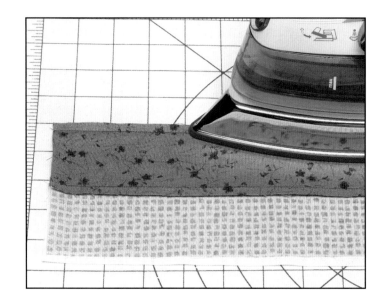

2. Open, and press toward seam, so seam is behind #2.

3. Continue to set just sewn seams and press strips open.

4. Stack in order.

5. Check on wrong side to see that all seams are going in same direction.

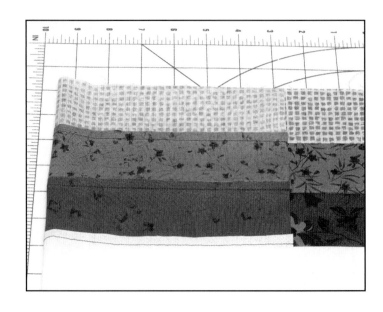

Sewing Sets of Four Together

1. From stack, place top set #5/1/2/3 to left. Arrange remaining sets in order.

2. Flip #4/5/6/7 right sides together to #5/1/2/3 and sew.

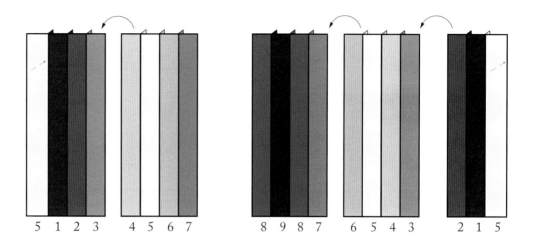

5   1   2   3   4   5   6   7   8   9   8   7   6   5   4   3   2   1   5

3. Continue to assembly-line sew sets into one unit.

4. Press just sewn seams in same direction as other seams.

5. Check seams from wrong side.

Cutting 2½" Sections

1. Fold in half right sides together on #9.

2. Place on cutting mat with fold across bottom.

3. Square off and straighten left end.

4. Cut 2½" sections.

Number of 2½" Sections	
Crib	7
Lap	7
Twin	9
Queen	7
King	7

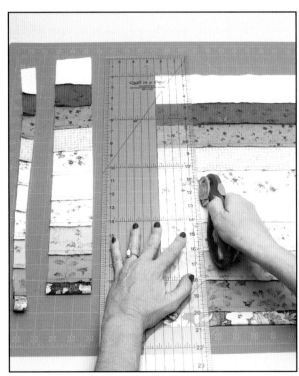

Cutting 2½" strips with 6" x 24" ruler and cutter.

5. Open up strips.

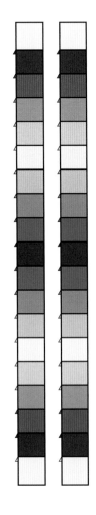

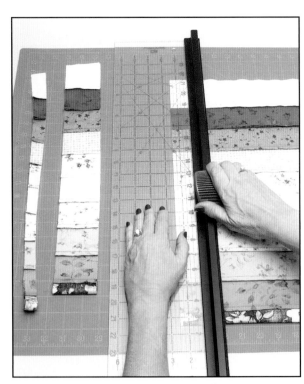

Cutting 2½" strips with ruler/cutter combo.

Sewing Center Together

1. Make two equal stacks. Set one section aside. Turn seams going **down on left stack**. Turn seams going **up on right stack**.

NUMBER IN EACH STACK	
Crib	3 in each
Lap	3 in each
Twin	4 in each
Queen	3 in each
King	3 in each

2. Off-set right stack by dropping it down one square.

3. Flip section on right to section on left.

4. Lock seams, pushing top seams up, and bottom seams down.

5. Sew a few inches, open and check that seams line up.

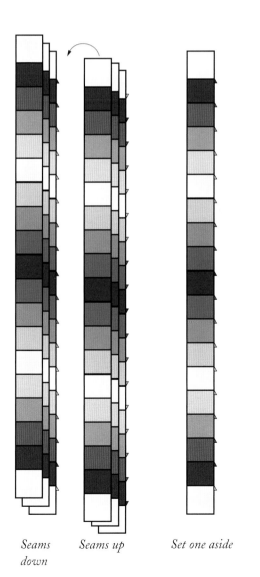

Seams down *Seams up* *Set one aside*

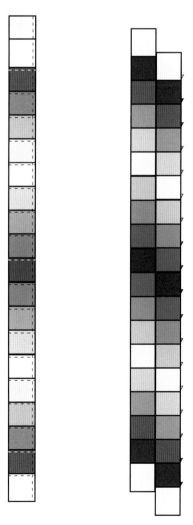

31

6. Sew pairs together, offsetting them one square, and locking seams.

7. Turn set aside section with seams going down. Sew to one pair offsetting one square.

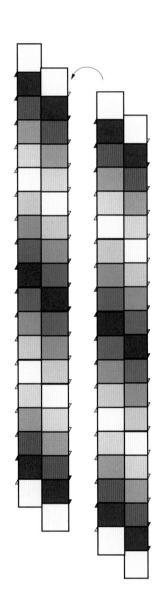

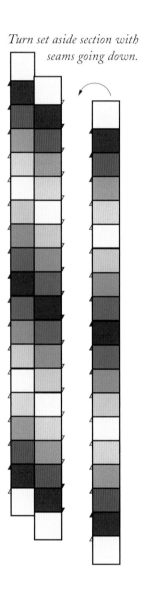

Turn set aside section with seams going down.

8. Sew sets together.

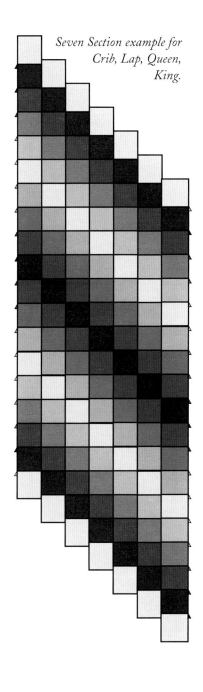

Seven Section example for Crib, Lap, Queen, King.

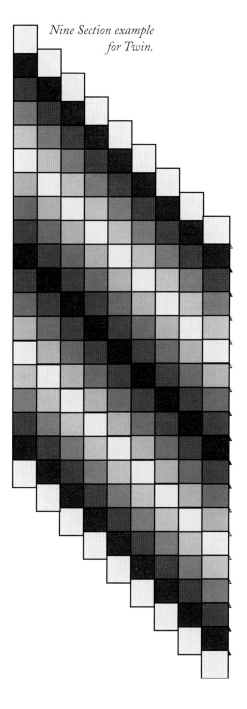

Nine Section example for Twin.

9. From wrong side, press seams flat from center strip out.

10. Press from center out on right side.

11. Set aside.

Example for Crib, Lap, Queen, King

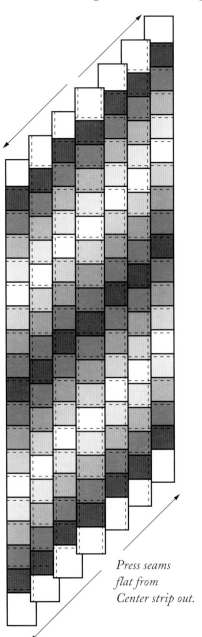

Press seams flat from Center strip out.

Example for Twin

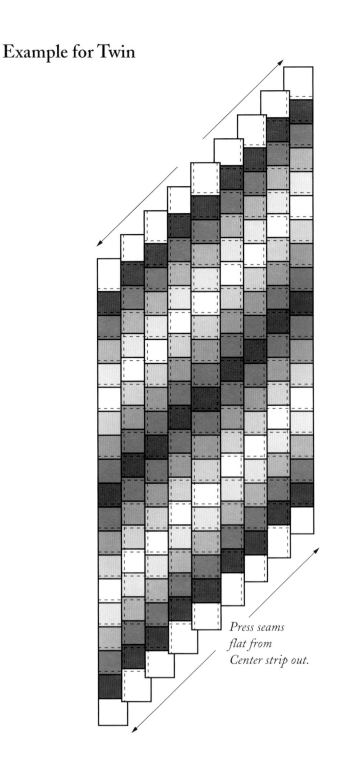

Press seams flat from Center strip out.

Sewing Remaining Strips

1. Count out **half strips** equally for each stack.

   You should have an extra half strip of #9.

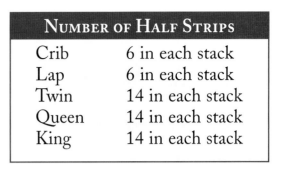

NUMBER OF HALF STRIPS	
Crib	6 in each stack
Lap	6 in each stack
Twin	14 in each stack
Queen	14 in each stack
King	14 in each stack

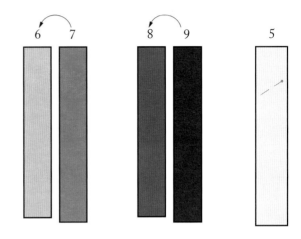

There are half strips in each stack.

2. Lay stacks in order with 2¾" strips of #5 in first and last positions. Place cut edge across top.

3. Divide into pairs. Set right stack of 2¾" strips of #5 aside.

4. Flip #1 strip on right to #5 strip on left.

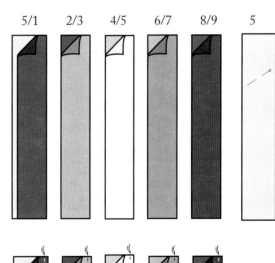

5. Assembly-line sew all #5/1 pairs right sides together.

6. Continue to assembly-line sew pairs together.

7. Clip apart and stack separate pairs in order.

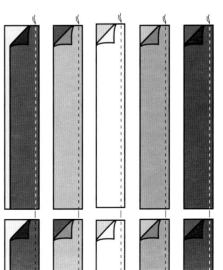

Half of the strips are now pressed in one direction, and half are pressed in the other direction for locking seams.

Sewing Left Set of Strips

1. Count out alike pairs in stacks.

NUMBER OF PAIRS	
Crib	3 pairs of each
Lap	3 pairs of each
Twin	7 pairs of each
Queen	7 pairs of each
King	7 pairs of each

2. Stack with 1, 3, 5, 7, and 9 on top.

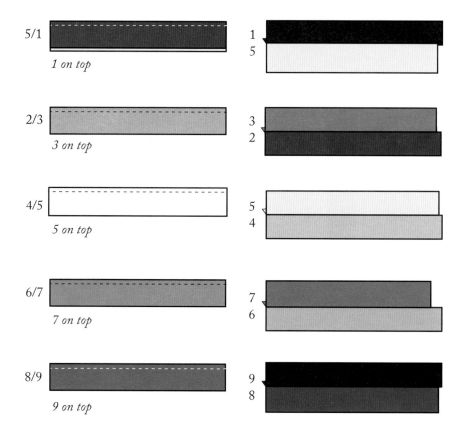

5/1
1 on top
1
5

2/3
3 on top
3
2

4/5
5 on top
5
4

6/7
7 on top
7
6

8/9
9 on top
9
8

3. Place pairs on pressing mat with seams across top. **Cut edge is on the left, and selvage is on the right.** Set seams.

4. Open, and press seams toward 1, 3, 5, 7, and 9.

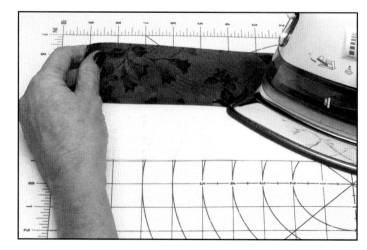

5. Sew pairs into sets of four.
   Sew 2¾" strip #5 to #8/9.
   Clip apart in order.

6. Set just sewn seams with stitching across the top, open, and
   press.

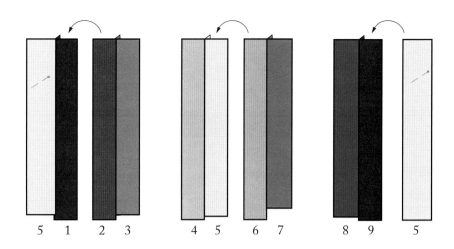

| 5 | 1 | 2 | 3 | | 4 | 5 | 6 | 7 | | 8 | 9 | 5 |

7. Sew three sets together.

8. Set just sewn seams with stitching
   across the top, open, and press.

9. **Seams should all go in same direction
   toward #9/5, or Second Color Family.**

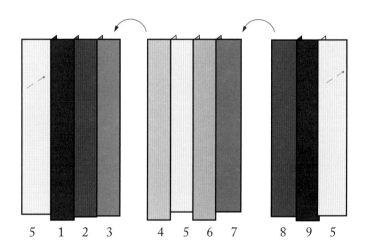

| 5 | 1 | 2 | 3 | | 4 | 5 | 6 | 7 | | 8 | 9 | 5 |

10. Turn over and check from wrong side.
    Make certain there are no folds or tucks
    at seams.

11. Stack, **mark as Left set,** and set aside.

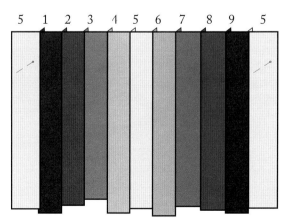

Seams are pressed toward #9/5, or Second Color Family.

Sewing Right Set Of Strips

1. Count out alike pairs of each, and turn over.

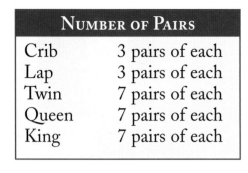

NUMBER OF PAIRS	
Crib	3 pairs of each
Lap	3 pairs of each
Twin	7 pairs of each
Queen	7 pairs of each
King	7 pairs of each

2. Stack with 5, 2, 4, 6, and 8 on top.

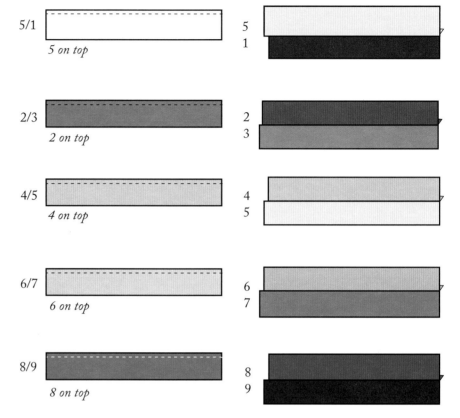

5/1
5 on top
5
1

2/3
2 on top
2
3

4/5
4 on top
4
5

6/7
6 on top
6
7

8/9
8 on top
8
9

3. Place pairs on pressing mat with seams across top. **Selvage is on left, and cut edge is on right.** Set seams.

4. Open, and press seams toward 5, 2, 4, 6, and 8.

5. Assembly-line sew pairs into sets of four. Sew 2¾" strip #5 to #8/9. Clip apart in order.

6. **Turn sets over.**

7. Set just sewn seams with **selvage on left, and cut edge on right**. Open, and press.

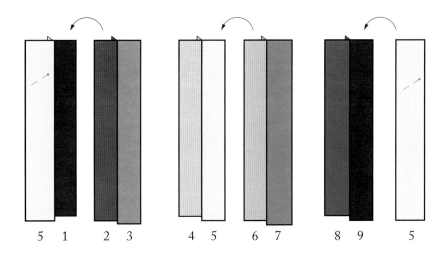

5 1   2 3   4 5   6 7   8 9   5

8. Sew the three sets together.

9. **Turn sets over.** Set just sewn seams with **selvage on left, and cut edge on right**. Open, and press.

10. **Seams should all go in same direction toward #5/1, or First Color Family.**

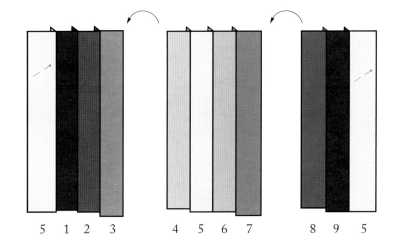

5 1 2 3   4 5 6 7   8 9 5

11. Turn over and check from wrong side. Make certain there are no folds or tucks at seams.

12. Stack, mark **as Right set,** and set aside.

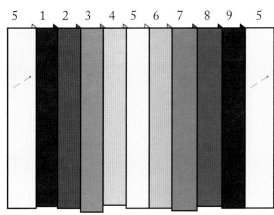

5 1 2 3 4 5 6 7 8 9 5

Seams are pressed toward #5/1, or first Color Family.

Cutting Sets into 2½" Strips

1. Place one from **Left Set** on cutting mat. If you are confident with your cutting skills, layer two at a time. Straighten left edge.

2. Cut all **Left Sets** into 2½" strips, and stack.

   You should get eight 2½" strips from each set.

NUMBER OF 2½" STRIPS FROM LEFT SET	
Crib	18 strips
Lap	18 strips
Twin	52 strips
Queen	56 strips
King	56 strips

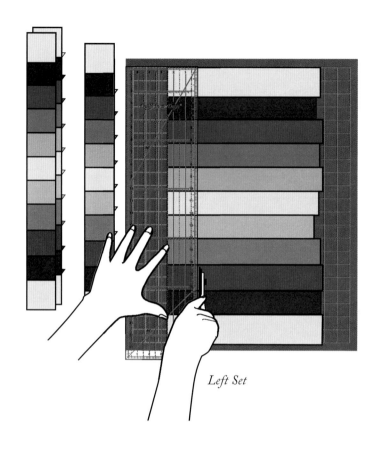

Left Set

3. Place **Right Set** on cutting mat. Straighten left edge.

4. Cut all **Right Sets** into 2½" strips, and stack in second pile.

5. Keep two separate stacks.

NUMBER OF 2½" STRIPS FROM RIGHT SET	
Crib	18 strips
Lap	18 strips
Twin	52 strips
Queen	56 strips
King	56 strips

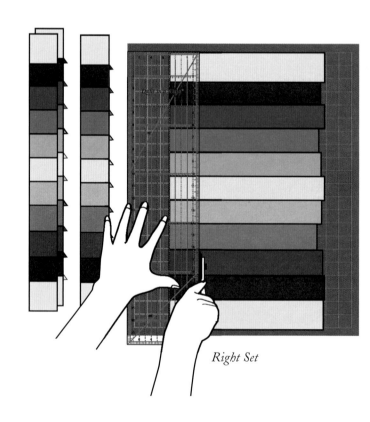

Right Set

Making Center Ends

A seam in each strip set is now "unsewn" and magically turned into two Center Ends. Left over strips are sewn into four Wide Seminole Corners!
(Crib quilt and Lap Corner pieces can be sewn into a bonus square quilt or pillow.)

Either a seam ripper or rotary cutter can be used for removing stitches. However, unsewing the seams with a small rotary cutter is extremely quick. Use a small rotary cutter that can be manually opened and closed. The type that needs downward pressure to expose the blade is not suitable.

Practice this Technique for "Unsewing" with a Rotary Cutter

1. Hold the rotary cutter with your thumb and forefinger in your right hand as you would hold a spoon or fork. Rest your wrist on the table.

2. Hold the fabric with the thumb and forefinger of your left hand near the seam to be unsewn.

3. Pull tension onto the fabric with the remaining three fingers of your right hand.

Take two strips from Left Set and "unsew" between #8 and #9.

4. With both hands tugging in opposite directions, pull the seam apart, exposing the thread.

5. Keeping your fingers out of the way, drop the rotary blade against the stitches and cut the thread as you pull.

6. Pick out the stitches in the seam allowance. Try "dabbing" the threads with cellophane tape for quick removal.

Take two strips from Right Set and "unsew" between #7 and #8.

Unsewing Two Center Ends

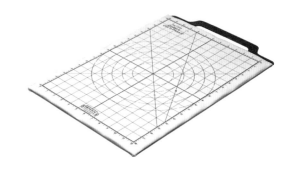

1. Clear **pressing mat** for laying out Center Ends. Turn in vertical position.

2. Count out 18 strips from Left Set and 18 strips from Right Set. Turn both stacks with #5/9 toward center.

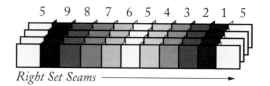

Left Set Seams ⟶   *Right Set Seams* ⟶

3. Take **two strips** from Left Set and "unsew" between #8 and #9. (See photos on page 41). Stack longest sections in Left Row One on pressing mat. (See next page).

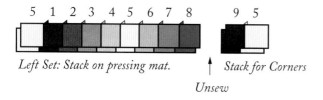

Left Set: Stack on pressing mat.   ↑ *Stack for Corners*
                                    Unsew

4. Stack shorter #9/5 for Corners. *(See below.)*

5. Take **two strips** from Right Set and "unsew" between #7 and #8. Stack longest sections in Right Row One. (See next page).

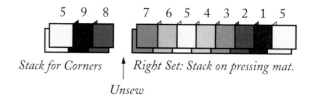

Stack for Corners ↑ *Right Set: Stack on pressing mat.*
            Unsew

6. Add shorter #5/9/8 to stack for Corners. Keep in order.

7. Following chart on next page, continue to take two sets from each side and "unsew". Stack in designated row for Center Ends.

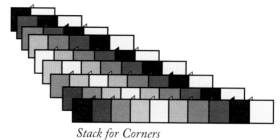

Stack for Corners

8. Stack unsewn pieces in order for Seminole Corners and set aside for instructions on page 49.

Center Ends

Refer to your Paste-Up Sheet.
If you make a mistake, sew pieces back together before proceeding.

Turn Second Color Family to center

Row One

| 5 | 1 | 2 | 3 | 4 | 5 | 6 | 7 | 8 |

Left - unsew between 8 and 9

| 7 | 6 | 5 | 4 | 3 | 2 | 1 | 5 |

Right - unsew between 7 and 8

Row Two

| 5 | 1 | 2 | 3 | 4 | 5 | 6 | 7 |

Left - unsew between 7 and 8

| 6 | 5 | 4 | 3 | 2 | 1 | 5 |

Right - unsew between 6 and 7

Row Three

| 5 | 1 | 2 | 3 | 4 | 5 | 6 |

Left - unsew between 6 and 7

| 5 | 4 | 3 | 2 | 1 | 5 |

Right - unsew between 5 and 6

Row Four

| 5 | 1 | 2 | 3 | 4 | 5 |

Left - unsew between 5 and 6

| 4 | 3 | 2 | 1 | 5 |

Right - unsew between 4 and 5

Row Five

| 5 | 1 | 2 | 3 | 4 |

Left - unsew between 4 and 5

| 3 | 2 | 1 | 5 |

Right - unsew between 3 and 4

Row Six

| 5 | 1 | 2 | 3 |

Left - unsew between 3 and 4

| 2 | 1 | 5 |

Right - unsew between 2 and 3

Row Seven

| 5 | 1 | 2 |

Left - unsew between 2 and 3

| 1 | 5 |

Right - unsew between 2 and 1

Row Eight

| 5 | 1 |

Left - unsew between 1 and 2

| 5 |

Right - unsew between 1 and 5

Row Nine

| 5 |

Left - unsew between 5 and 1

Remaining two are used later
on page 49.

43

Sewing Two Center Ends

1. On the end of each strip, pull out threads and press where seams had been unsewn. Keep rows in order as you press.

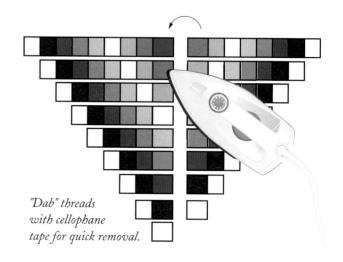

"Dab" threads with cellophane tape for quick removal.

2. **Work on one set of strips at a time.** Flip strips on right to strips on left. Assembly-line sew.

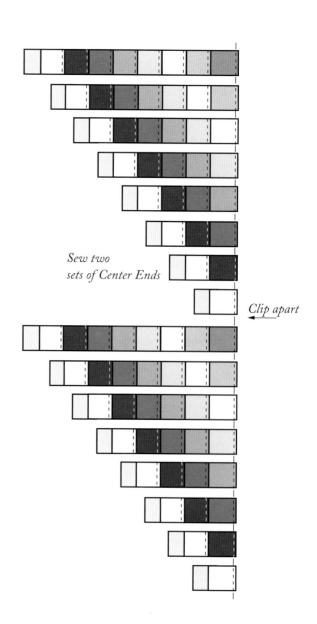

Sew two sets of Center Ends

Clip apart

3. Clip two sections apart.

4. Lay on pressing mat with just sewn seams across top. Set just sewn seams, open, and press against seams. **Seams go in same direction as other seams in strip.**

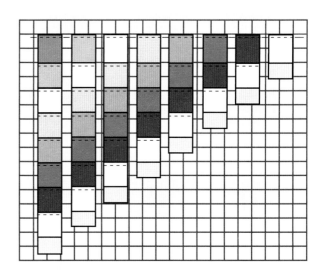

5. **Lay out one** for Bottom Center End, **wrong side up**. Clip connecting threads.

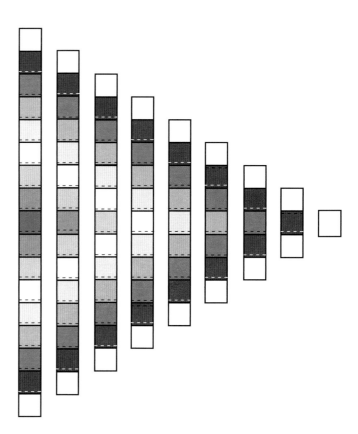

Making Bottom Center End

Seams go in opposite directions on Bottom and Top Center Ends so seams lock with Center.

1. **In the Bottom Center End,** turn strips with seams going down in Rows One, Three, Five, and Seven.

2. Turn strips with seams going up in Rows Two, Four, Six, and Eight.

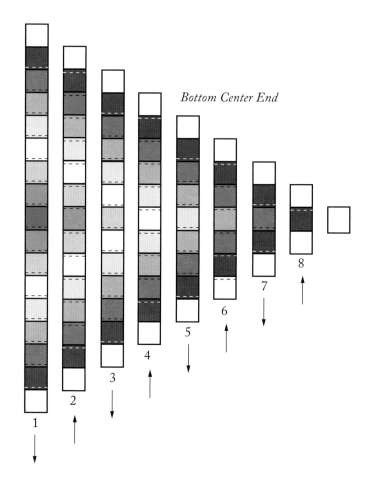

Bottom Center End

3. **Turn strips right sides up,** keeping them in order. Divide into pairs.

4. Assembly-line sew all rows into pairs, keeping new strips one step lower than previous strip. Match and lock seams.

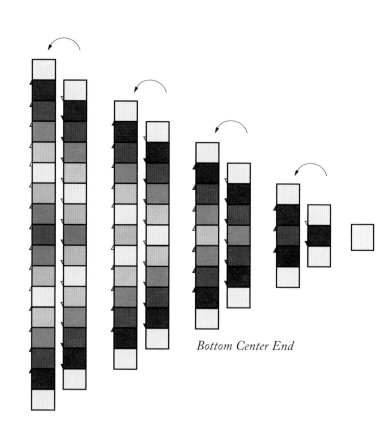

Bottom Center End

5. Assembly-line sew pairs together.

6. Carefully center 2¾" side of single piece of #5, and sew.

7. Label as Bottom Center End, and set aside.

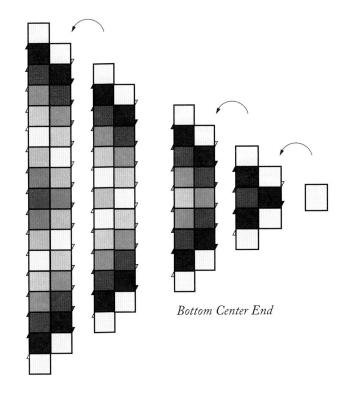

Bottom Center End

Making Top Center End

Seams are opposite in Top Center End.

1. Lay out remaining set for Top Center, wrong side up. Clip connecting threads.

2. **In the Top Center End,** turn strips with seams going up in Rows One, Three, Five, and Seven.

3. Turn strips with seams going down in Rows Two, Four, Six, and Eight so seams lock together when sewn.

4. Turn all strips right sides up, keeping them in order. Divide into pairs.

5. Assembly-line sew together, keeping strips one square lower than previous strip.

6. Add 2¾" single piece of #5.

7. Label as Top Center End.

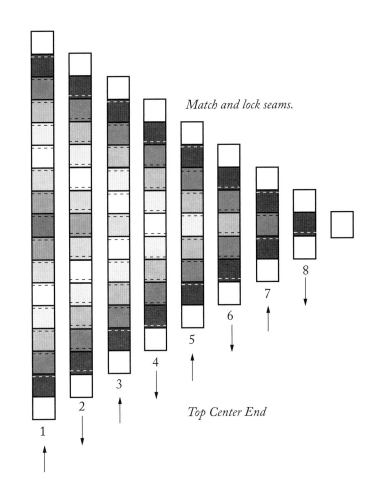

Match and lock seams.

Top Center End

Sewing Center Together

1. Place Center on table.

2. Place Top and Bottom Center Ends. Check that seams are going in opposite directions with Center seams.

3. Sew Ends to Center, locking seams.

4. On wrong side, **press seams from center strip out.**

5. Press from right side.

Top Center End

Bottom Center End

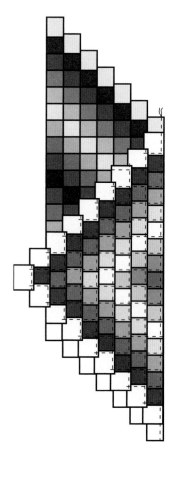

Crib and Lap Quilt:
Strips unsewn for Corners are not needed to finish your quilt. However, strips can be sewn together for a Bonus Wallhanging or Floor Pillow (page 91).

Crib:
Skip to page 56 to trim your Boston Common quilt.

Lap Quilt:
Skip to page 65 and make your narrow Seminole Border.

48

Making Four Corners for Wide Seminole Border

1. Turn pressing mat in horizontal position, and place pieces set aside for corners on mat.

2. Cut 2¾" strip of #5 into (4) 2¾" squares. Place in Row 10 position.

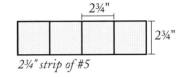

2¾"

2¾"

2¾" strip of #5

3. Take two Right Set strips left over from Center Ends. Unsew between #9 and #8.

4. Stack shortest sections in Row Nine. **The long piece is extra. Set aside.**

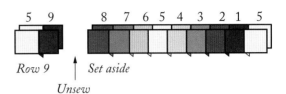

5 9

8 7 6 5 4 3 2 1 5

Row 9   *Set aside*

Unsew

Strips must be laid out with longest strip on left.

5. Sort pieces for Corners. Place four alike strips **wrong side up** in each row.

6. Turn Rows One, Three, Five, Seven, and Nine with seams down. *Two strips need to be re-pressed so Corner seams lock together with Seminole Border.*

7. Turn Rows Two, Four, Six, and Eight with seams up. *Two strips need to be re-pressed.*

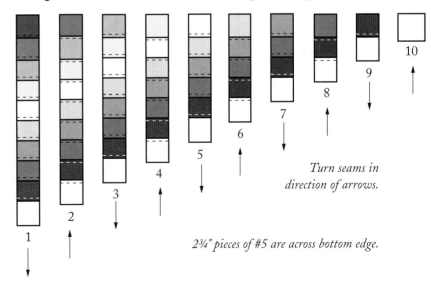

Turn seams in direction of arrows.

2¾" pieces of #5 are across bottom edge.

8. Turn strips right sides up. Line up top edge, and divide into pairs.

9. Working with one pair at a time, flip right sides together.

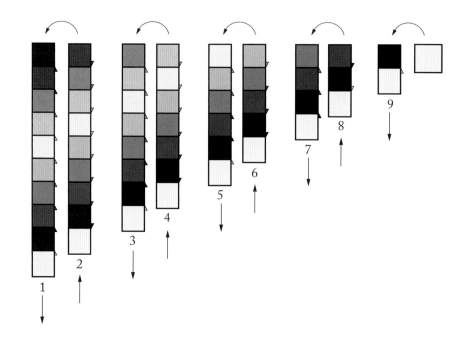

10. Assembly-line sew like pairs together, locking seams. Clip apart and stack in order. **Do not press.**

11. Open pairs and assembly-line sew together.

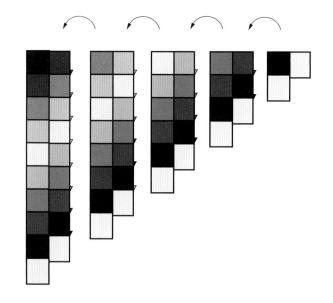

Pressing Four Corners for Quilt

1. All four Corners are pressed the same way.

2. From wrong side, press all seams toward Row One.

3. Press from right side.

Crib and Lap: Sew four Corners into Bonus Wallhanging or Pillow. Directions are on page 91.

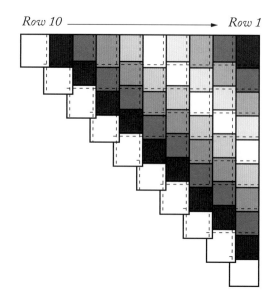

Row 10 ⟶ *Row 1*

Making a Wide Seminole Border

1. Count out equal 2½" strips from left and right sets.

NUMBER OF STRIPS	
Twin	36 strips from each
Queen	38 strips from each
King	38 strips from each

2. Stack 2½" strips from left set with seams down.

3. Stack 2½" strips from right stack with seams up. Place stack on right one square lower than one on left.

4. Assembly-line sew pairs together, locking seams.

5. Clip pairs apart.

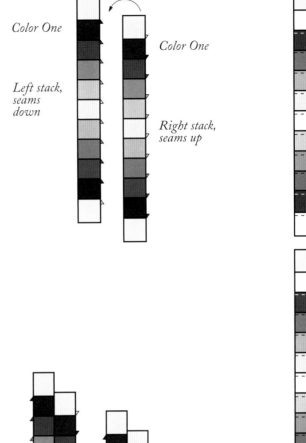

Color One

Left stack, seams down

Color One

Right stack, seams up

6. **Set pairs aside.**

NUMBER OF SET ASIDE PAIRS	
Twin	4 pairs
Queen	2 pairs
King	2 pairs

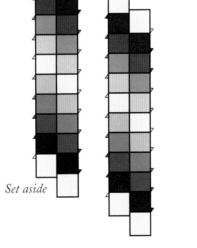

Set aside

7. Assembly-line sew remaining pairs into sets of four.

NUMBER OF SETS OF FOUR	
Twin	16 sets of four
Queen	18 sets of four
King	18 sets of four

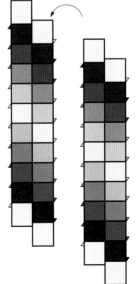

Making Top and Bottom for Wide Seminole Border

1. Count out designated sets of four plus pairs if needed.

2. Assembly-line sew together one for Top and one for Bottom.

NUMBER OF SETS FOR TOP AND BOTTOM	
Twin	3 sets of four plus one pair
Queen	4 sets of four
King	4 sets of four

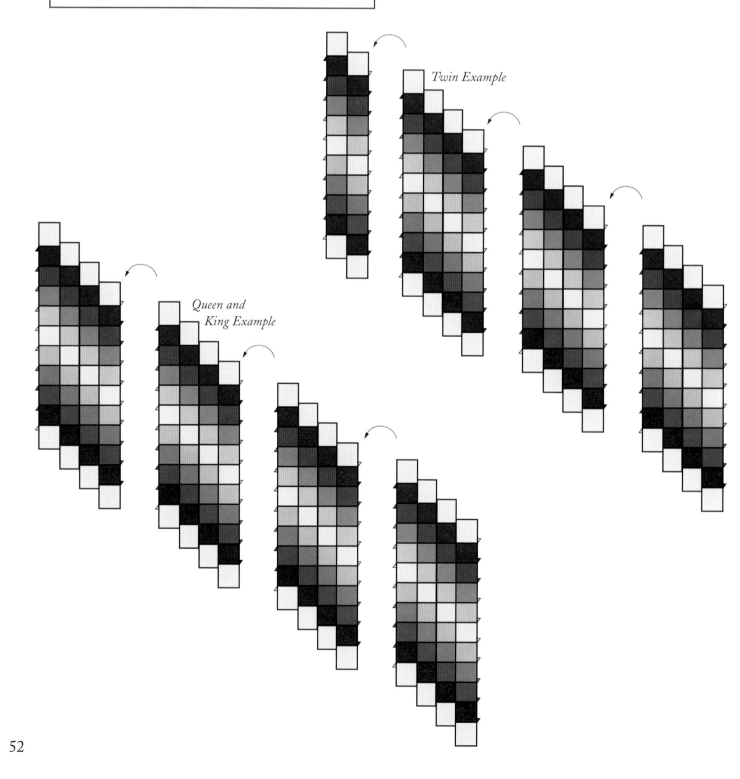

Twin Example

Queen and King Example

Making Sides for Wide Seminole Borders

1. Count out designated sets of four plus one pair.

2. Assembly-line sew together one for Left Side and one for Right Side.

3. Sew one pair to each.

NUMBER OF SETS FOR EACH SIDE	
Twin	5 sets of four plus one pair
Queen	5 sets of four plus one pair
King	5 sets of four plus one pair

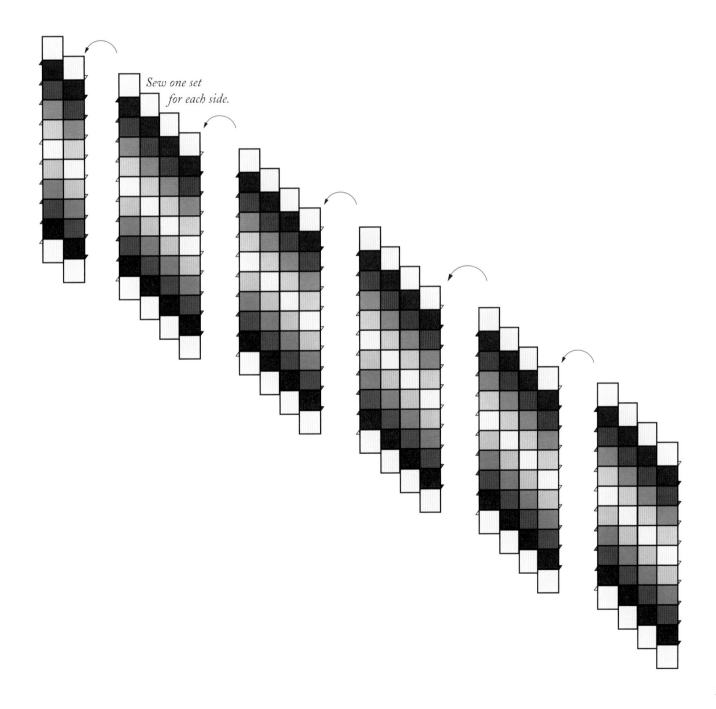

Sew one set for each side.

Wide Seminole Border

1. Lay out Corners with Seminole Borders.

2. Place Corners on end of each strip.
   Flip right sides together. Lock seams.
   Background is ¼" longer on end.

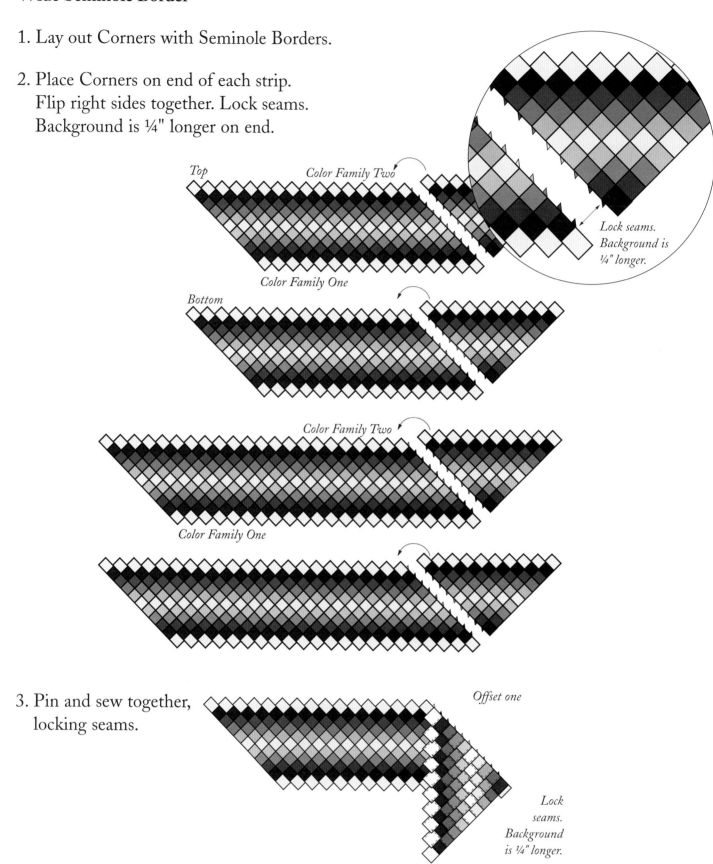

Top

Color Family Two

Lock seams. Background is ¼" longer.

Color Family One

Bottom

Color Family Two

Color Family One

3. Pin and sew together, locking seams.

Offset one

Lock seams. Background is ¼" longer.

Pressing Seminole Seams

1. Turn Seminole pieces **wrong side up.**

2. From wrong side, press seams in one short Seminole to right. Press from right side in same direction seams are going. Label as **Top Seminole** and set aside.

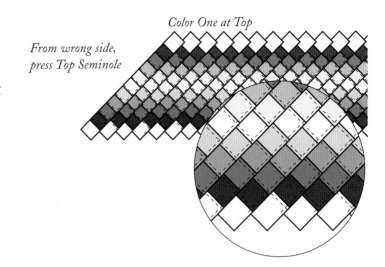

Color One at Top

From wrong side, press Top Seminole

3. From wrong side, press seams in remaining short Seminole to left. Press from right side in same direction seams are going. Label as **Bottom Seminole** and set aside.

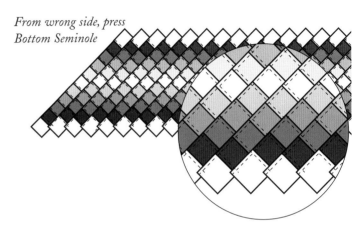

From wrong side, press Bottom Seminole

4. From wrong side, press seams in one long Seminole to right. Press from right side in same direction seams are going. Label as **Right Seminole** and set aside.

From wrong side, press Right Seminole seams to right.

5. From wrong side, press seams in one long Seminole to left. Press from right side in same direction seams are going. Label as **Left Seminole** and set aside.

From wrong side, press Left Seminole seams to left.

Sewing Top Together

Trimming Edges of Center

1. Place 12½" or 16" Square Up ruler with 45° line on corner. Line up ruler's diagonal line down center of strip, and outside quarter inch lines with seams. **If necessary, manipulate fabric under ruler.**

2. Trim four corners.

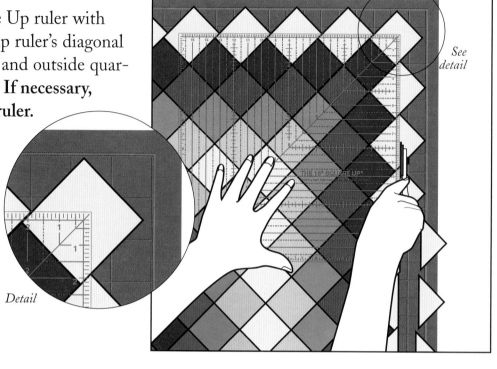

Detail

See detail

3. Trim remaining tips on sides with 6" x 24" ruler. Line up quarter inch lines on ruler with seams, and trim ¼" away from seam.

Crib: Skip to page 80 to finish your quilt.

Detail

See detail

Trimming Wide Seminole Border

1. Place 6" x 24" ruler on **inside** edge of Wide Seminole Border, or Color Family One. Line up quarter inch line on ruler with peaks of seams, and trim ¼" away. **Outside corners are trimmed to peaks because there is no seam.**

2. Trimmed edges are on the bias. *Be very careful not to stretch. Do not drape Seminole Borders over table while trimming or measuring.*

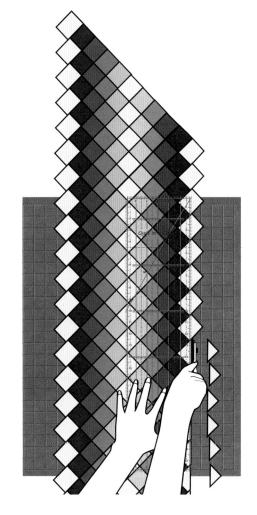

3. **It's critical that the outside corners are trimmed as illustrated because there is no seam.**

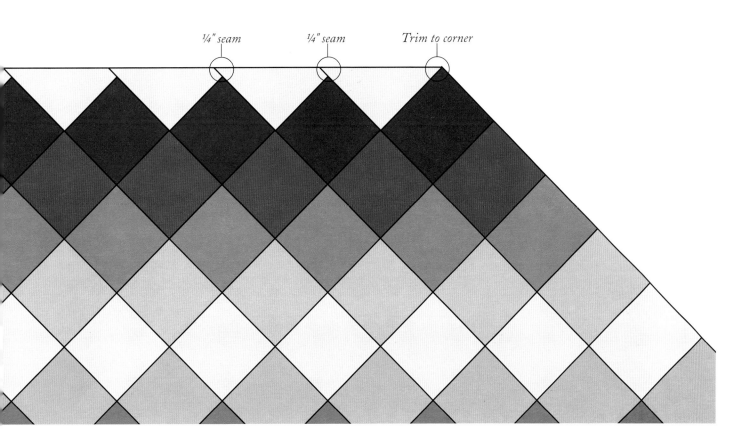

¼" seam   ¼" seam   *Trim to corner*

Calculating Width of Inside Border Strips

1. Place in positions on large table or floor area.

2. Measure pieces as illustrated with 72" tape measure, or 72" yardstick. Check measurement on opposite side. If measurements are different, add two together, and divide the total by two for an average measurement.

3. Record measurements and follow steps to find how wide to cut Inside Border strips. Measurements are based on your personal seam allowance.

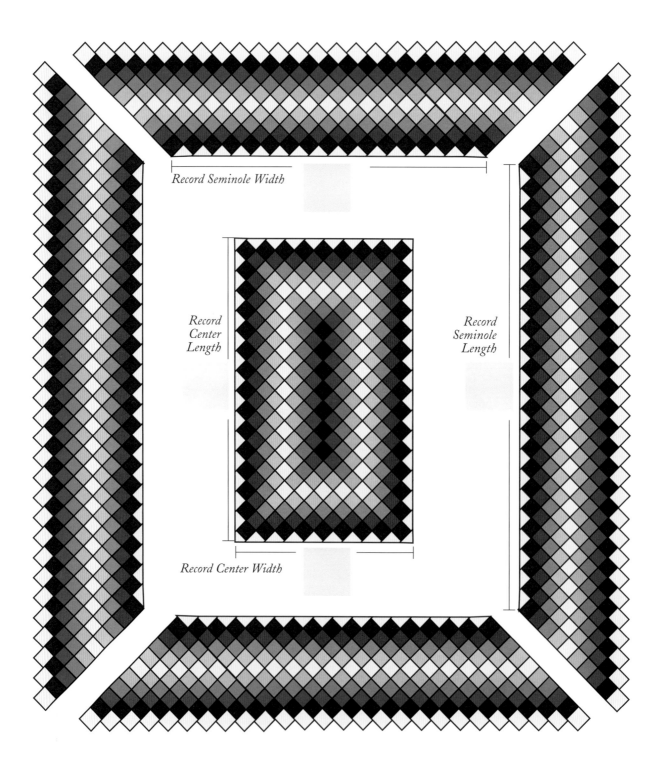

Record Seminole Width

Record Center Length

Record Seminole Length

Record Center Width

Fill in these spaces to find your own personal width for Inside Border strips. Yours may differ slightly from the example. Widths of strips for Sides and Top and Bottom may not always be the same.

Strip Width for Sides

	Twin Example	*Queen & King Example*	*Your Measurement*
Seminole Width	39½"	45"	___ "
Center Width	−25½"	− 25"	− ___ "
	= 14"	= 20"	= ___ "
Divide by Two	÷ 2	÷ 2	÷ 2
	= 7"	= 10"	= ___ "
Add ½" for Seams	+ ½"	+ ½"	+ ½"
Side Strip Width	= 7½"	=10½"	= ___ "

Strip Width for Top and Bottom

	Twin Example	*Queen & King Example*	*Your Measurement*
Seminole Length	62"	62"	___ "
Center Length	− 47"	− 42"	− ___ "
Difference	= 15"	= 20"	= ___ "
Divide by Two	÷ 2	÷ 2	÷ 2
	= 7½"	= 10"	= ___ "
Add ½" for Seams	+ ½"	+ ½"	+ ½"
Top and Bottom Strip Width	= 8"	=10½"	= ___ "

Sewing Inside Border Strips to Center

1. Cut Inside Border strips according to calculated width for Sides. (Page 59).

Number of Side Strips	
Twin	3 (piece together)
Queen	2
King	2

2. Cut strips to Center length. (Page 58).
   If strips are pieced, place seams away from ends.

3. Place Center right sides together to Inside Border strip, with Center on top. Pat Center to fit and pin at every point.

4. Sew ¼" seam with Center on bottom.
   Trimmed edges are on bias, and stretch less when sewn on the bottom next to the feed dogs.

5. Set seam with Inside Border on top, open, and press against seam toward Border.

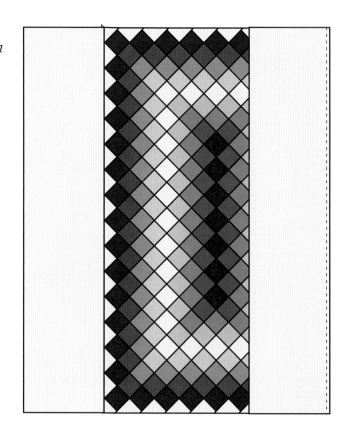

6. Cut Inside Border strips according to calculated width for Top and Bottom strips. (Page 59)

Strips Top and Bottom	
Twin	2
Queen	3 (piece together)
King	3 (piece together)

7. Measure from edge to edge. Cut two pieces that size. *If strips are pieced, place seams away from sides.*

8. Place Center right sides together to Top and Bottom Inside Border Strips.

9. Pat edges flat, pin at every point, and sew.

10. Set seam with Inside Border strip on top, open, and press against seam.

If you prefer not to have a seam, cut strips lengthwise.

Check to see if you can get four strips across the width of your fabric and you have enough length.

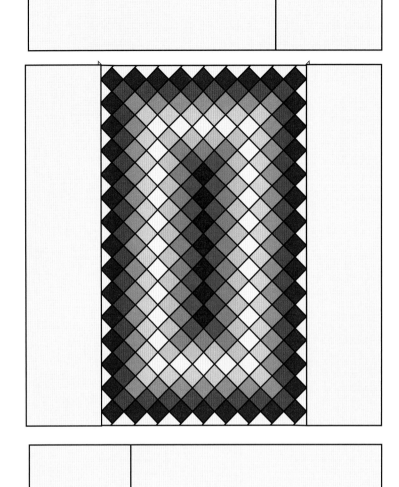

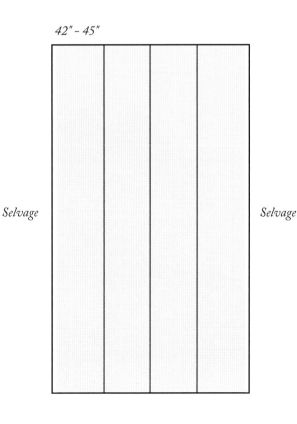

42" - 45"

Selvage

Selvage

Sewing Wide Seminole Border to Quilt Top

1. On the right side of the quilt top, mark a dot ¼" from each corner. Place a pin mid-point on each side.

2. On the wrong side of Seminole Border ends, mark a dot at the ¼" point on the seam line.

3. Place a pin midpoint on each.

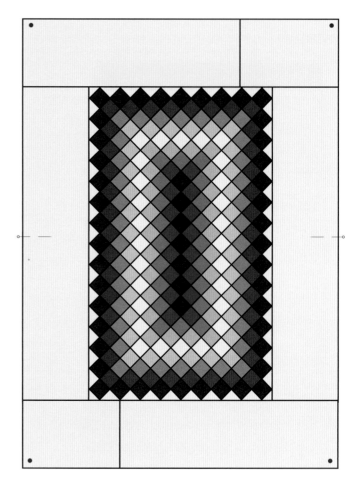

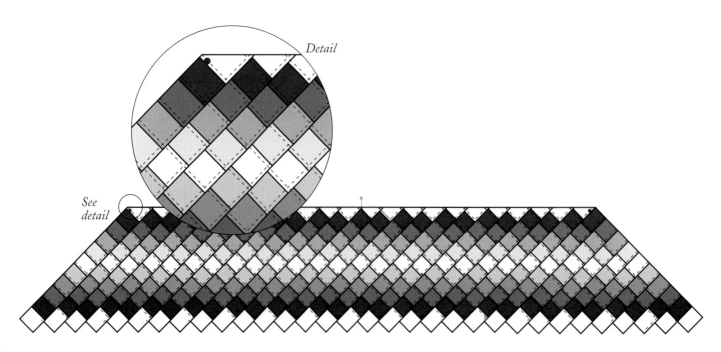

Detail

See detail

4. Lay quilt right side up on a flat surface. Pin Seminole Border midpoint right sides together to quilt midpoint.

5. Match and pin dots at each end.

6. Pin every seam the way they are pressed. "Pat" Seminole flat to Inside Border. Ease or stretch slightly if necessary.

7. Pin the opposite Seminole to the quilt top.

8. Working from the Inside Border side, backstitch to the corner dot and then sew to the dot at the other end, and backstitch again. Repeat for opposite side.

Do not stitch past marked dots into seam allowance. This will cause a tuck at the corner.

9. Gently press seams toward Inside Border.

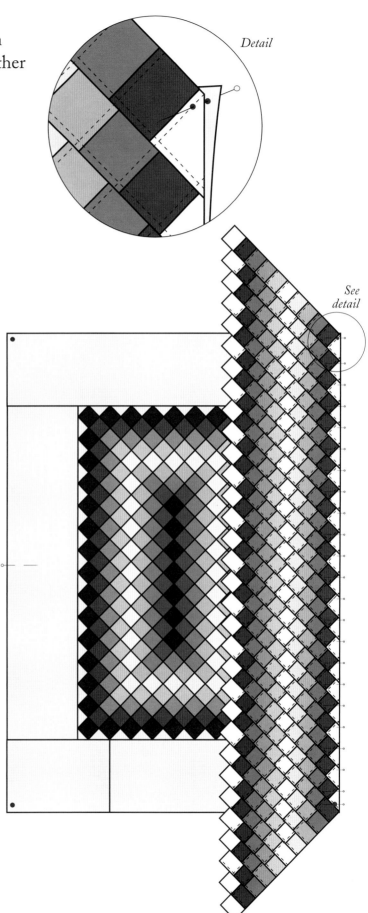

Detail

See detail

10. Match and pin remaining two Seminole Borders.

11. Backstitch and sew.

12. Press seams toward Inside Border.

13. Match seams and pin the mitered corner.

14. Backstitch to the corner mark and sew to the outer edge.

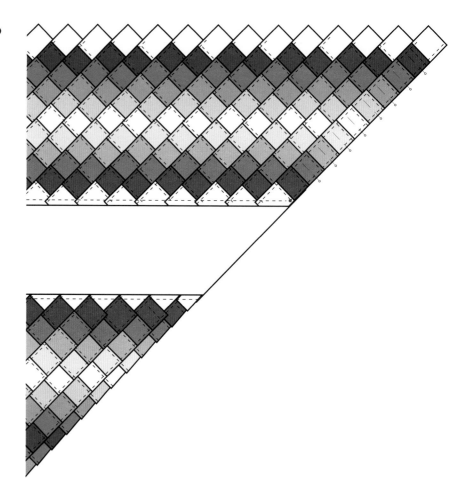

15. Press mitered corner seam open.

16. Place 12½" or 16" Square Up ruler with 45° line on corner. Line up ruler's diagonal line down center of strip, and outside quarter inch lines with seams. **If necessary, manipulate fabric under ruler.**

17. Trim four corners.

18. Trim remaining tips on sides with 6" x 24" ruler. Line up quarter inch lines on ruler with seams, and trim ¼" away from seam.

Twin, Queen:
Turn to page 80 to finish your quilt.

Making Narrow Seminole for Lap and King Only

First Color Family

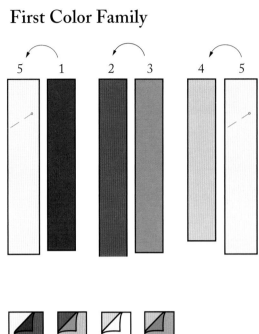

1. Count out half strips for each stack.

NUMBER OF HALF STRIPS		
Lap	12	half strips
King	20	half strips

2. Lay out stacks of strips in order with 2¾" strips of #5 in first and last positions. Place cut edge at top, and selvage edge at bottom.

3. Divide into pairs. Work on one set of pairs at a time. Flip strip on right to strip on left.

4. Assembly-line sew pairs right sides together.

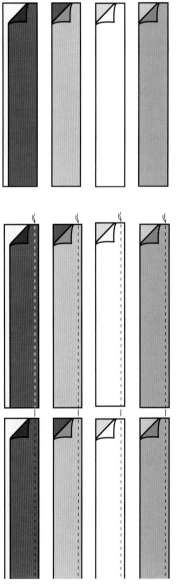

Sewing Left Set of Strips

Half of the strips are now pressed in one direction,
and half are pressed in the other direction for locking seams.

1. Count out equal pairs of each.
   Stack with 1, 3, and 5 on top.

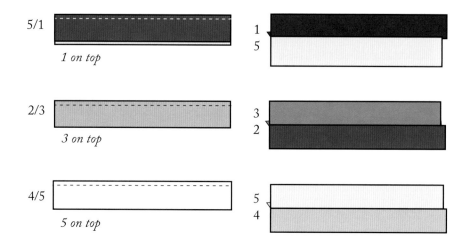

5/1 — *1 on top*

2/3 — *3 on top*

4/5 — *5 on top*

NUMBER OF PAIRS	
Lap	6 pairs
King	10 pairs

2. Place pairs on pressing mat
   with seams across top. **Cut
   edge is on the left, and selvage
   is on the right.**

3. Set seams, open, and press
   seams toward 1, 3, and 5.

4. Sew pairs into sets of six.

5. Set just sewn seams, open, and press.

**Seams should all go in same direction
toward #4/5.**

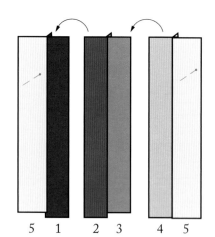

5   1   2   3   4   5

6. Turn over and press from right side against
   seams, making certain there are no folds or
   tucks at seams.

7. Stack, mark as **Left set**, and set aside.

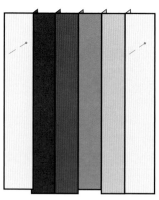

Seams are pressed toward #4/5

Sewing Right Set Of Strips

1. Count out remaining pairs of each, and **turn over**. Stack with 5, 2, and 4 on top.

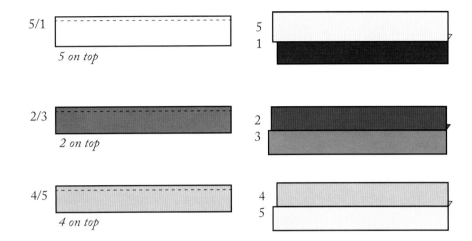

NUMBER OF PAIRS	
Lap	6 pairs
King	10 pairs

2. Place pairs on pressing mat with seams across top. **Selvage is on left, and cut edge is on right.**

3. Set seams, open, and press seams toward 5, 2, and 4.

4. Sew pairs into sets of six. **Turn sets over.**

5. Set just sewn seams with selvage on left, and cut edge on right. Open, and press.

   Seams should all go in same direction toward #5/1.

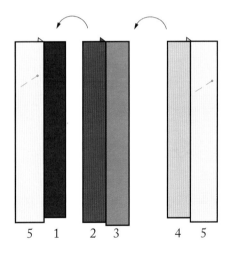

6. Turn over and press from right side against seams, making certain there are no folds or tucks at seams.

7. Stack, mark as **Right set**, and set aside.

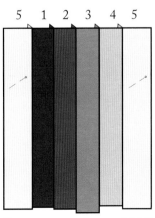

Seams are pressed toward #5/1

Cutting Sets into 2½" Strips

1. Place one from **Left Set** on cutting mat. If you are confident with your cutting skills, layer two at a time. Straighten left edge.

2. Cut all **Left Sets** into 2½" strips, and stack.

Number From Left Set	
Lap	42
King	74

You should get eight 2½" strips from each set.

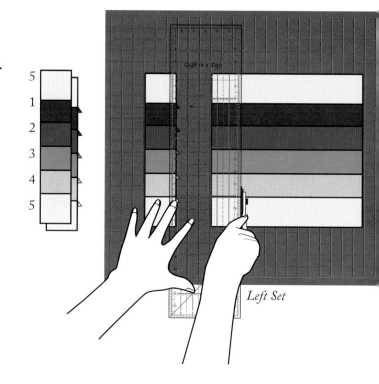

Left Set

3. Place **Right Set** on cutting mat. Straighten left edge.

4. Cut all **Right Sets** into 2½" strips, and stack in second pile.

Number From Right Set	
Lap	42
King	74

5. Keep two separate stacks.

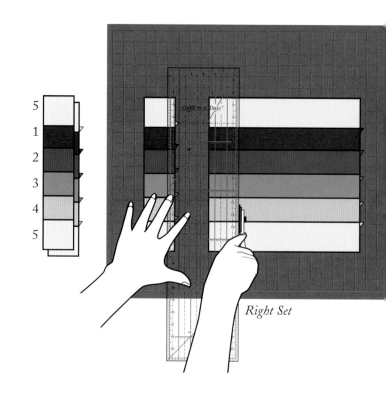

Right Set

Making Four Corners for Narrow Seminole Border

1. Stack eight strips from Left set and eight strips from Right set.

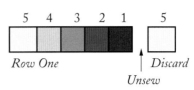

Left Set   *Right Set*

2. Take four strips from Left set and unsew between #1 and #5. Stack all four longer strips in Row One. *(See below)* Discard #5 piece.

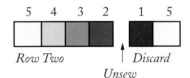

Row One   *Discard*
Unsew

3. Take four strips from Right set and unsew between #1 and #2. Stack all four longer strips in Row Two. Discard #1/5.

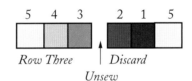

Row Two   *Discard*
Unsew

4. Take four strips from Left set and unsew between #2 and #3. Stack four #5/4/3 in Row Three. Discard #2/1/5.

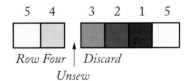

Row Three   *Discard*
Unsew

5. Take four strips from Right set and unsew between #3 and #4. Stack four #5/4 in Row Four. Discard #3/2/1/5.

5 4   3 2 1 5

Row Four | *Discard*
Unsew

6. Cut (4) 2¾" squares from 2¾" strip and place in Row 5.

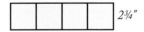

2¾"

7. Place pieces **wrong side up** in each row.

8. Turn Rows One and Three with seams down. *Corner seams lock together with Seminole Border.*

9. Turn Rows Two and Four with seams up.

1   2   3   4   5

10. Turn strips right sides up.
    Line up top edge, and divide
    into pairs.

11. Flip pairs right sides together, and sew.

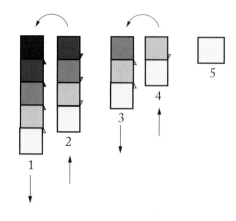

12. Assembly-line sew together,
    locking seams.

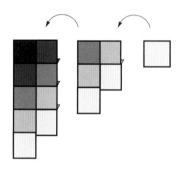

Pressing Four Corners

1. All four Corners are pressed the same way.

2. From wrong side, press all seams toward
   Row One.

3. Press from right side.

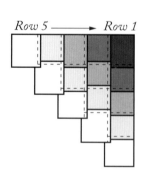

Sewing Strips Together

1. Stack 2½" strips from left stack, placing **seams down**.

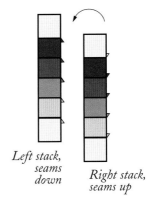

Left stack,
seams
down

Right stack,
seams up

2. Stack 2½" strips from right stack, placing **seams up**. Place stack on right one square lower than one on left.

NUMBER OF 2½" STRIPS		
Lap	34	strips
King	66	strips

3. Assembly-line sew pairs together, locking seams.

4. Clip pairs apart.

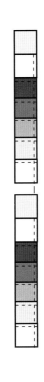

5. **Set two pairs aside.**

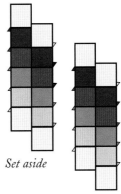

Set aside

6. Assembly-line sew remaining pairs into sets of four.

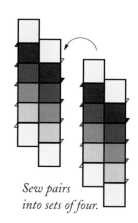

Sew pairs into sets of four.

NUMBER OF SETS OF FOUR		
Lap	16	sets of four
King	32	sets of four

Making Top and Bottom for Narrow Seminole Border

1. Count out sets of four for Top and sets of four for Bottom and assembly-line sew together.

2. Sew one pair to Top, and one pair to Bottom.

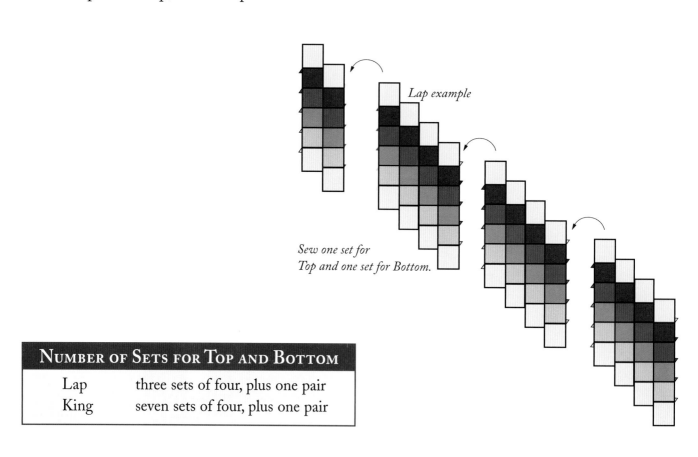

Lap example

Sew one set for Top and one set for Bottom.

NUMBER OF SETS FOR TOP AND BOTTOM	
Lap	three sets of four, plus one pair
King	seven sets of four, plus one pair

Making Two Long Sides for Narrow Seminole Borders

1. Count out sets of four for each Side.

2. Assembly-line sew together.

NUMBER OF SETS FOR SIDES	
Lap	five sets of four
King	nine sets of four

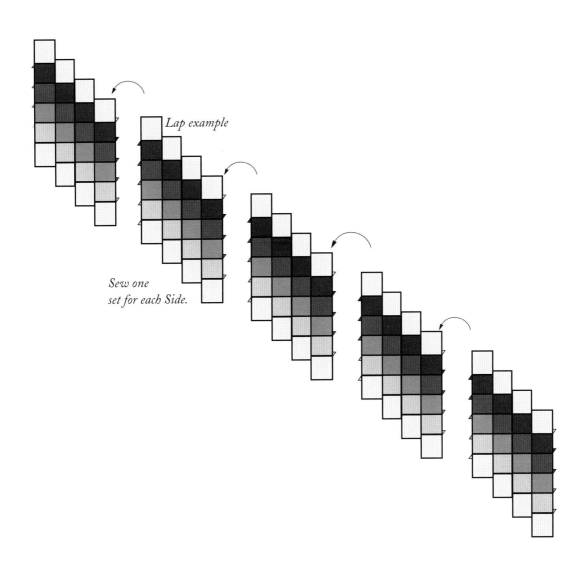

Lap example

Sew one set for each Side.

Narrow Seminole Border

1. Lay out Corners with Seminole Borders.

2. Place Corners on end of each strip.
   Flip right sides together. Match seams.
   Background is ¼" longer.

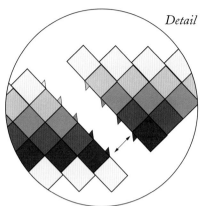

Detail

Match seams.
Background is ¼" longer.

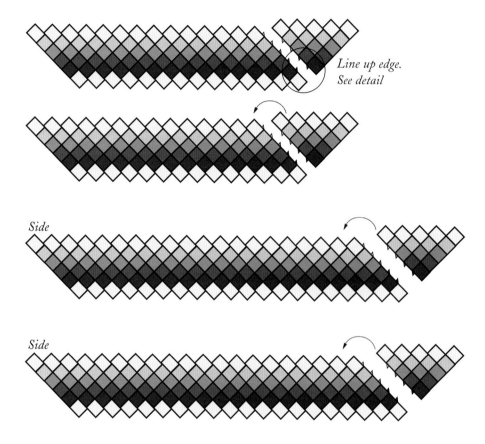

Line up edge.
See detail

Side

Side

3. Pin and sew together, locking seams.

Offset one

Background
is ¼" longer.

Pressing Seminole Seams

1. Turn Seminole pieces **wrong side up.**

2. From wrong side, press seams in one short Seminole to right. Press from right side. Label as **Top Seminole** and set aside.

3. From wrong side, press seams in one long Seminole to right. Press from right side. Label as **Right Seminole** and set aside.

From wrong side, press Top and Right Seminole seams to right.

4. From wrong side, press seams in remaining short Seminole to left. Press from right side. Label as **Bottom Seminole** and set aside.

5. From wrong side, press seams in one long Seminole to left. Press from right side. Label as **Left Seminole** and set aside.

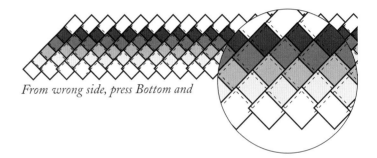

From wrong side, press Bottom and

Trimming Narrow Seminole Border

1. Place 6" x 24" ruler on **inside** edge of Narrow Seminole Border. Line up quarter inch line on ruler with seams, and trim ¼" away from seams. **Trim outside corners to peaks.**

2. Trimmed edges are on the bias. *Be very careful not to stretch. Do not drape Seminole Borders over table while trimming or measuring.*

3. **Lap:** Trim edges of Center as on page 56. Then turn to page 76 to continue.

4. **King:** Trim edges of Wide Seminole Border as on page 57, then turn to page 78 to continue.

Lap

Calculating Width of Inside Border Strips

1. Place in position on large table or floor area.

2. Measure pieces as illustrated with 72" tape measure, or 72" yardstick. Check measurement on opposite side. If measurements are different, add two together, and divide the total by two for an average measurement.

3. Record measurements and follow steps to find how wide to cut Inside Border strips. Measurements are based on your personal seam allowance.

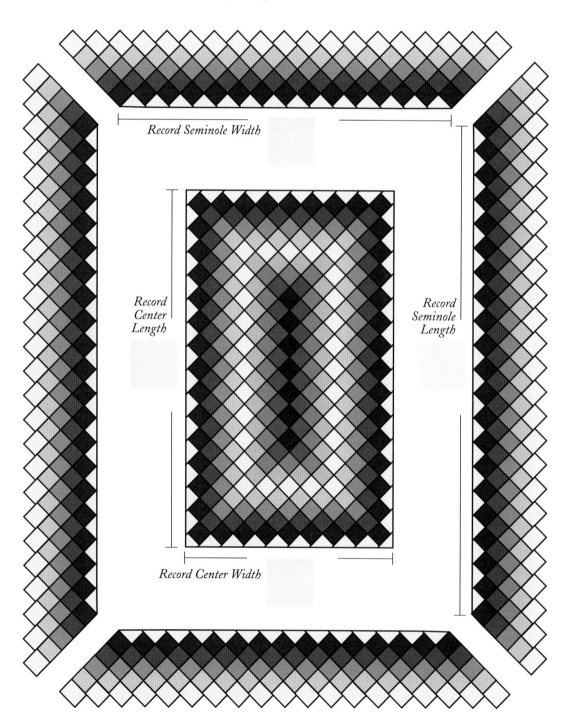

Record Seminole Width

Record Center Length

Record Seminole Length

Record Center Width

Fill in these spaces to find your own personal width for Inside Border strips. Yours may differ slightly from the example. Widths of strips for Sides and Top and Bottom may not always be the same. Sew together following directions starting on page 60. Narrow Seminole Border is sewn to quilt top with same technique as Wide Seminole Border.

Strip Width for Sides

	Lap Example	*Your Measurement*
Seminole Width	40"	"
Center Width	− 25"	− ___ "
	= 15"	= ___ "
Divide by Two	÷ 2	÷ 2
	= 7½"	= ___ "
Add ½" for Seams	+ ½"	+ ½"
Side Strip Width Cut two strips this measurement	= 8"	= ___ "

Strip Width for Top and Bottom

	Lap Example	*Your Measurement*
Seminole Length	57"	"
Center Length	− 42"	− ___ "
Difference	= 15"	= ___ "
Divide by Two	÷ 2	÷ 2
	= 7½"	= ___ "
Add ½" for Seams	+ ½"	+ ½"
Top and Bottom Strip Width Cut two strips this measurement	= 8"	= ___ "

King

Calculating Width of Second Inside Border Strips

1. Place in positions on large table or floor area.

2. Measure pieces as illustrated with 72" tape measure, or 72" yardstick. Check measurement on opposite side. If measurements are different, add two together, and divide the total by two for an average measurement.

3. Record measurements and follow steps to find how wide to cut Inside Border strips. Measurements are based on your personal seam allowance.

Record Seminole Width

Record Center Length

Record Seminole Length

Record Center Width

Fill in these spaces to find your own personal width for Inside Border strips. Yours may differ slightly from the example. Widths of strips for Sides and Top and Bottom may not always be the same. Sew Narrow Seminole to quilt top with same technique as Wide Seminole.

Strip Width for Sides

	King Example	Your Measurement
Seminole Width	85½"	"
Center Width	- 73½"	- _____ "
	= 12"	= "
Divide by Two	÷ 2	÷ _____ 2
	= 6"	= "
Add ½" for Seams	+ ½"	+ _____ ½"
Side Strip Width Cut four strips this measurement	= 6½"	= "

Strip Width for Top and Bottom

	King Example	Your Measurement
Seminole Length	103½"	"
Center Length	- 90"	- _____ "
Difference	= 13½"	= "
Divide by Two	÷ 2	÷ _____ 2
	= 6¾"	= "
Add ½" for Seams	+ ½"	+ _____ ½"
Top and Bottom Strip Width Cut four strips this measurement	= 7¼"	= "

Finishing Your Quilt

Piecing Border Strips for Larger Quilts

1. Square off selvage edges.

2. Lay first strip right side up. Lay second strip right sides to it. Backstitch, stitch and back stitch again.

3. Continue assembly-line sewing all short ends together into one long piece.

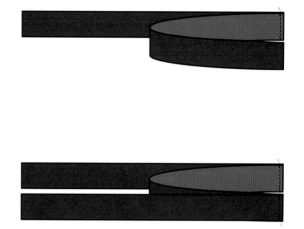

Adding Borders

1. If necessary, trim remaining tips from Seminole Borders, page 57.

2. Cut two pieces the average length of left and right sides.

3. Pin and sew to sides. Set seams with Border on top. Open, and press seams toward Border.

4. Measure width and cut Border pieces for top and bottom.

5. Pin and sew to quilt. Set seams, open, and press toward Border.

6. Add remaining Borders.

Layering the Quilt

1. Spread out Backing on a large table or floor area, right side down. Clamp fabric to edge of table with quilt clips, or tape Backing to the floor. Do not stretch Backing.

2. Layer the Batting on the Backing and pat flat.

3. With quilt right side up, center on the Backing. Smooth until all layers are flat. Clamp or tape outside edges.

Red lines represent quilting paths.

Marking with Straight Lines
See quilting paths on quilt above .

1. Place 6" x 24" ruler through corners of one fabric. Firmly push Hera marker along edge of ruler, and mark crease.

2. Mark rectangles on every row of fabric, or every other row of fabric.

Safety Pinning

1. Place pin covers on 1" safety pins. Safety pin through all layers three to five inches apart. Pin away from marked quilting lines.

2. Catch tip of pin in grooves on pinning tool, and close pins.

3. Use pinning tool to open pins when removing them. Store pins opened.

"Stitch in the Ditch" with Walking Foot

1. Thread your machine with matching thread or invisible thread. If you use invisible thread, loosen top tension. Match the bobbin thread to the Backing.

2. Attach your walking foot, and lengthen the stitch to 8 to 10 stitches per inch or 3.5 on computerized machines.

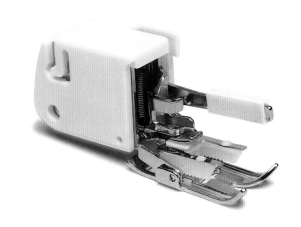

3. Place hands on quilt in triangular shape, and spread seams open. Stitch in the ditch around the Center Square.

4. Stitch continuously around each rectangle, pivoting and turning with needle down.

Quilting with Darning Foot

1. Select a stencil 2" narrower than Border areas. Center stencil on Borders, and trace lines with water erasable fabric marking pen.

2. Attach darning foot to sewing machine. Drop feed dogs or cover feed dogs with a plate. No stitch length is required as you control the length. Use a fine needle and invisible or regular thread in the top and regular thread to match the Backing in the bobbin. Loosen top tension if using invisible thread.

3. Place hands flat on sides of marking. Bring bobbin thread up on line. Lock stitch and clip thread tails. Free motion stitch around design. Lock stitch and cut threads.

4. Stitch on cable lines with darning or walking foot. Background can be filled in with stippling.

Example Stencil is #SCO-027-05.
Lines can be stitched with a walking foot or darning foot.

Measure width of Border. Draw line down center on four Borders. Draw centering lines on stencil. Measure cable from one dot to other. Example marked with dots is 6". Center stencil and mark four corners with water erasable pen. Measure from outside of one corner square to inside of opposite corner square. Divide by cable length. Example length is 44" divided by 6" to equal 7⅓". Cable will need to be elongated by 1⅓" to be equally spaced from one corner to other. Elongate by tracing first half, sliding stencil the difference needed, and tracing second half. Continue marking all cables with elongation.

Binding

Use a walking foot attachment and regular thread on top and in the bobbin to match the Binding.

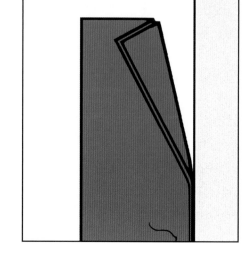

1. Square off the selvage edges, and sew 3" Binding strips together lengthwise. Fold and press in half with wrong sides together.

2. Line up raw edges of folded Binding with raw edges of quilt in middle of one side. Begin stitching 4" from the end of Binding. Stitch with 10 stitches per inch, or 3.0 to 3.5 stitch length on computerized machines. Sew ⅜" from edge, or width of walking foot.

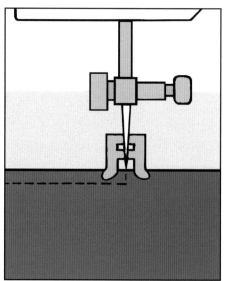

3. At the corner, stop the stitching ⅜" from the edge with the needle in the fabric. Raise the presser foot and turn the quilt to the next side. Put the foot back down.

4. Stitch backwards off the edge of the Binding, raise the foot, and pull the quilt forward slightly.

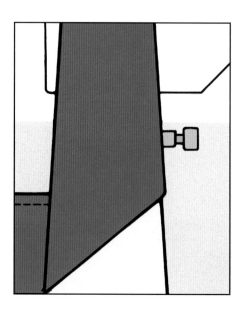

5. Fold the Binding strip straight up on the diagonal. Fingerpress the diagonal fold.

6. Fold the Binding strip straight down with the diagonal fold underneath. Line up the top of the fold with the raw edge of the Binding underneath.

7. Begin sewing from the edge.

8. Continue stitching and mitering the corners around the outside of the quilt.

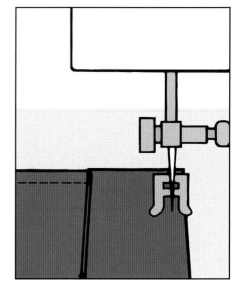

9. Stop stitching 4" from where the ends will overlap.

10. Line up the two ends of Binding. Trim the excess with a ½" overlap.

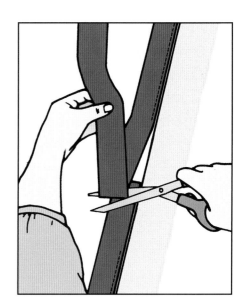

11. Open out the folded ends and pin right sides together. Sew a ¼" seam.

12. Continue to stitch the Binding in place.

13. Trim the Batting and Backing up to the raw edges of the Binding.

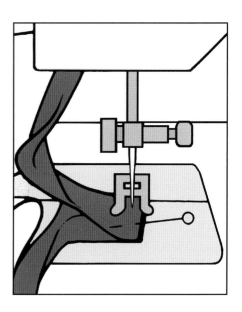

14. Fold the Binding to the back side of the quilt. Pin in place so that the folded edge on the Binding covers the stitching line. Tuck in the excess fabric at each miter on the diagonal.

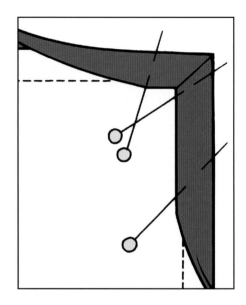

15. From the right side, "stitch in the ditch" using invisible thread on the front side, and a bobbin thread to match the Binding on the back side. Catch the folded edge of the Binding on the back side with the stitching.
Optional: Hand stitch Binding in place.

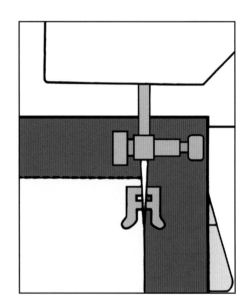

16. Sew an identification label on the Back. Embroidered labels make a nice touch. Eleanor Burn's embroidery memory card, "Quilting Labels Collection I," is available at www.amazingdesigns.com or you can call 888-874-6760 for a dealer near you.

Applique Instructions

Sew applique pieces on Inner Border before or after adding Seminole Borders.

Yardage for Flowers and Vine
Photograph of quilt on page 12

1 yd   Medium weight non-woven fusible interfacing

⅝ yd   Green for Leaves and Vine
Cut 20" square for Vines
Make 52 Leaves
Make 4 Calyx

¼ yd   Print for Flowers
Make 10 Flowers and 4 Buds

⅛ yd   Solid for Flowers
Make 10 Flowers

¼ yd   for Yo-yos
Make 10 Yo-yos from 3½" circles
Make 10 Yo-yos from 3" circles

Yardage for Oak Leaves and Acorns
Photograph of quilt on back inside cover

1 yd   Medium weight non-woven fusible interfacing

⅝ yd   Brown for Vine
Cut 20" square for Vines

¼ yd   Medium Green
Make 10 small leaves
Make 10 large leaves

¼ yd   Dark Green
Make 6 small leaves
Make 6 large leaves

⅛ yd   Top of Acorn
Make 24 tops

⅛ yd   Bottom of Acorn
Make 24 bottoms

1. Trace patterns on template plastic with template marking pen. Cut out shapes.

2. Turn non-woven fusible interfacing smooth side up. With permanent marking pen, trace around patterns on smooth side of interfacing with ½" space between each.

3. Place rough, fusible side of interfacing against right side of fabric. Pin. With 20 stitches per inch or 1.8 on computerized machines, sew on drawn lines.

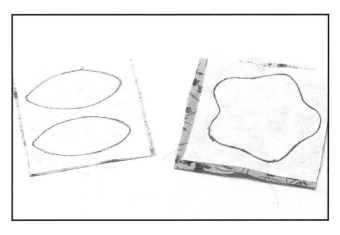

4. Trim seams to ⅛". Clip inside curves.

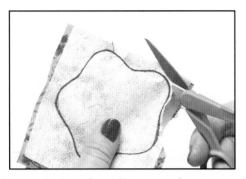

5. Cut small opening in center of interfacing. Insert straw into hole. Push straw against fabric.

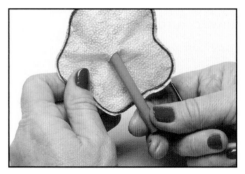

6. Place ball of bodkin on fabric stretched over straw. Gently push fabric into straw with bodkin, to turn piece.

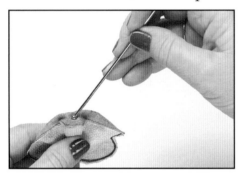

7. Remove straw and bodkin. Insert straw in second half, and turn right side out. Run bodkin around inside edge, pushing out seams.

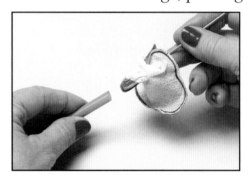

8. From right side, push fabric over interfacing edge with wooden iron.

9. Cut cotton batting same size as shape. Insert batting though opening with hemostat.

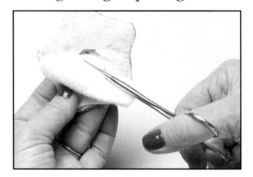

10. **Yo-yo:** Double thread hand sewing needle and knot the end.

11. Turn under edge ¼" to wrong side, and baste. Pull tight, push needle to back, and knot.

Making a Bias Vine

1. Line up 45° line on 6" x 24" ruler with left edge of 20" square.

2. Cut on diagonal. Fabric to left of cut can be used for Leaves.

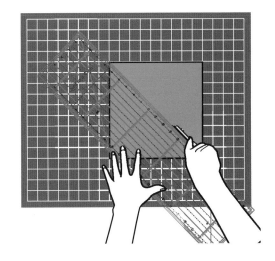

3. Move ruler over 1¼" from diagonal cut. Cut again.

4. Cut half of square into bias strips.

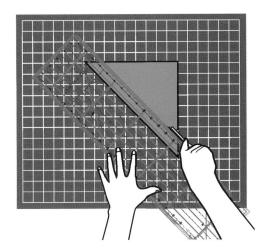

5. Piece bias strips together on angle until strip is approximately 6 yds long. Press seams open.

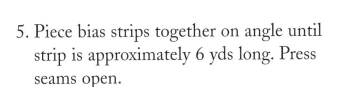

6. Press raw edges under with ½" bias tape maker.

7. Place Vine on Background Border beginning on one end. Turn direction of Vine every third square. Pin on both sides.

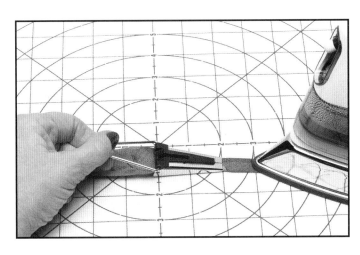

8. Topstitch or handstitch on both sides of Vine.

9. Place applique pieces on top, fuse in place, and hand or machine stitch around outside edges. Stitch yo-yo to center of flower.

Flower and Leaf

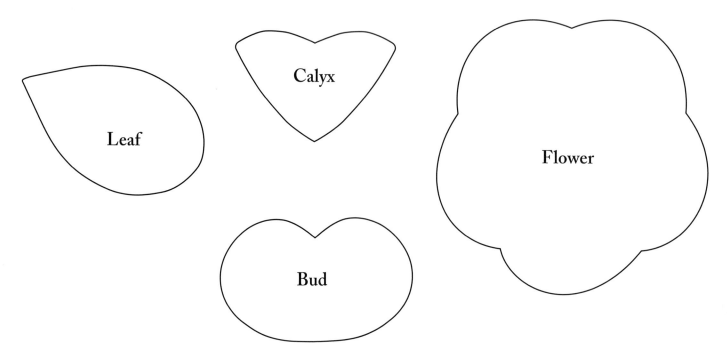

Oak Leaves and Acorns

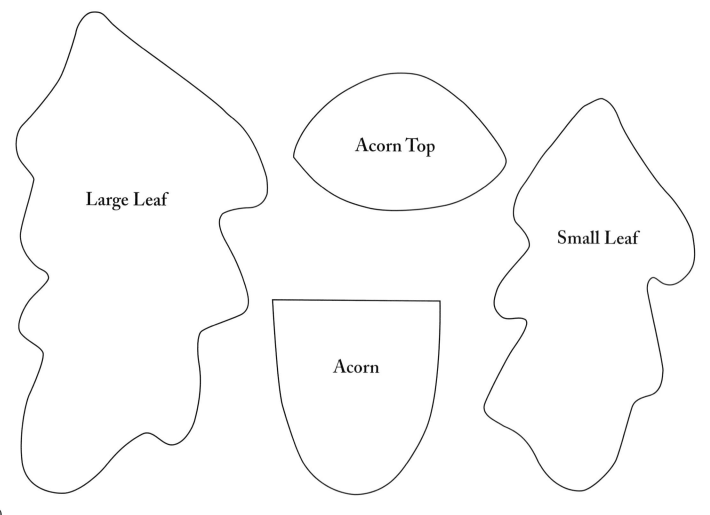

Bonus Wallhanging and Pillow

Teresa Varnes   39" x 39"

Teresa Varnes   27" x 27"

Additional Wallhanging Purchases

First Border   ⅓ yd
   (4) 2" strips
Second Border   ⅝ yd
   (4) 4½" strips
Binding   ½ yd
   (4) 3" strips

Backing   1 yd
Batting   45" x 45"

Additional Pillow Purchases

Backing   1 yd
Pillow Form   22" square

1. **Wallhanging and Pillow:** Make Four Corners (pages 49 - 50) and sew together into a square. Trim outside edges.

2. **Wallhanging:** Finish by following directions on pages 80 - 86.

3. **Pillow:** Cut two pieces 17" x 29". Press under 1" hem on long side, and edgestitch.

4. Pin Backing right sides together to Pillow Front, overlapping hemmed edges in center. Trim excess fabric.

5. Sew ¼" seam around outside edge, and turn right side out.

6. Sew 2½" in from outside edge to form edge and stuff.

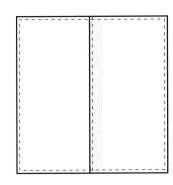

Duck

(12) 2½" left over strips
Backing   ½ yd
Thin Batting   18" x 45"
Stuffing   1 bag
⅜" Ribbon   ½ yd

Instructions

¼" Seam not included

1. Sew twelve left over strips together.

2. Layer with ½ yd backing and batting.

3. Quilt three layers together with stippling.

4. Trace duck pattern and cut out.

5. Place pattern on right side of fabric. Cut ¼" away from pattern for seam allowance.

6. **Flip pattern over** and place on left side of fabric. Cut mirror image duck ¼" away from pattern.

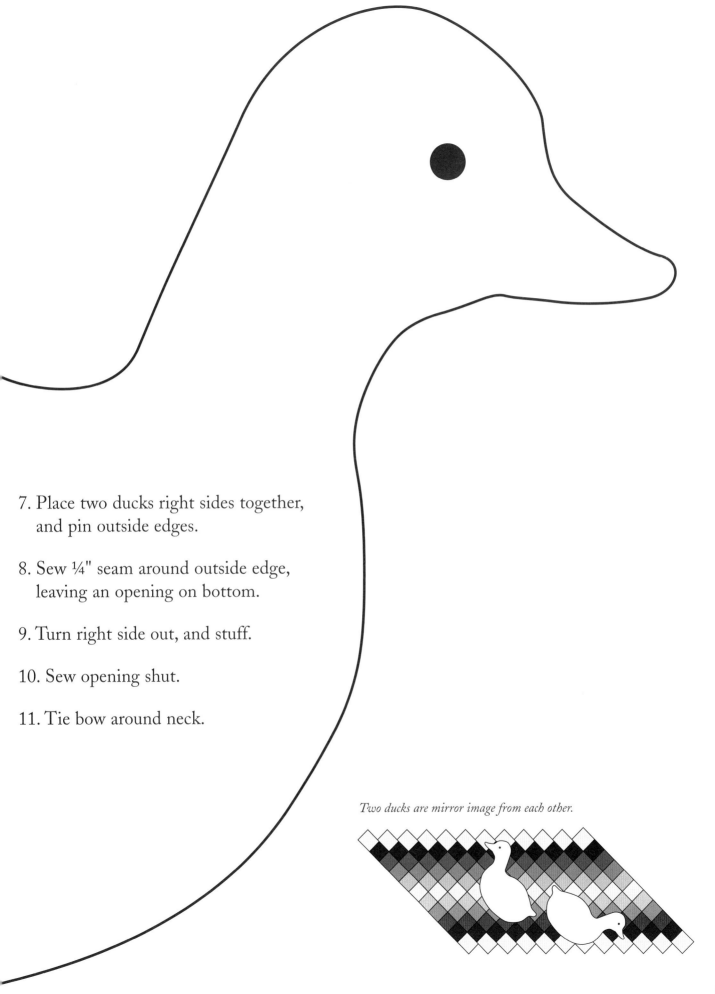

7. Place two ducks right sides together, and pin outside edges.

8. Sew ¼" seam around outside edge, leaving an opening on bottom.

9. Turn right side out, and stuff.

10. Sew opening shut.

11. Tie bow around neck.

Two ducks are mirror image from each other.

Index

Thank you to Margaret Conners

Sebastian Miniature made in Marblehead, Mass. Designed by Prescott W. Sasto

Cheers to all the quiltmakers

Sue Bouchard

Marie Harper

Carol Selepec

Sandy Thompson

Teresa Varnes

Order Information

Quilt in a Day books offer a wide range of techniques and are directed toward a variety of skill levels. If you do not have a quilt shop in your area, you may write or call for a complete catalog and current price list of all books and patterns published by Quilt in a Day®, Inc.

Easy

Make a Quilt in a Day Log Cabin
Irish Chain in a Day
Bits & Pieces Quilt
Trip Around the World Quilt
Heart's Delight Wallhanging
Rail Fence Quilt
Flying Geese Quilt
Star for all Seasons Placemats
Winning Hand Quilt
Courthouse Steps Quilt
Nana's Garden Quilt
Double Pinwheel
Easy Strip Tulip
Northern Star
Flying Geese Quilt in a Day

Applique

Applique in a Day
Dresden Plate Quilt
Sunbonnet Sue Visits Quilt in a Day
Country Cottages and More
Spools & Tools Wallhanging
Dutch Windmills Quilt
Grandmother's Garden Quilt
Ice Cream Cone Quilt

Intermediate

Trio of Treasured Quilts
Lover's Knot Quilt
Amish Quilt
May Basket Quilt
Morning Star Quilt
Friendship Quilt
Kaleidoscope Quilt
Machine Quilting Primer
Star Log Cabin Quilt
Snowball Quilt

Tulip Table Runner
Jewel Box
Triple Irish Chain Quilts
Bears in the Woods
Wild Goose Chase Quilt
Birds in the Air Quilt
Delectable Mountains Quilt

Holiday

Christmas Quilts and Crafts
Country Christmas
Bunnies & Blossoms
Patchwork Santa
Last Minute Gifts
Angel of Antiquity
Log Cabin Wreath Wallhanging
Log Cabin Christmas Tree Wallhanging
Country Flag
Lover's Knot Placemats
Stockings & Small Quilts

Sampler

The Sampler
Block Party Series 1, Quilter's Year
Block Party Series 2, Baskets & Flowers
Block Party Series 3, Quilters Almanac
Block Party Series 4, Christmas Traditions
Block Party Series 5, Pioneer Sampler
Block Party Series 6, Applique in a Day
Block Party Series 7, Stars Across America
Town Square Sampler

Angle Piecing

Diamond Log Cabin Tablecloth or Treeskirt
Pineapple Quilt
Blazing Star Tablecloth
Schoolhouse Quilt
Radiant Star Quilt

Quilt in a Day®, Inc. • 1955 Diamond Street • San Marcos, CA 92069
1 800 777-4852 • Fax: (760) 591-4424 • www.quiltinaday.com

This becoming Boston Common quilt looks festive set against a crisp winter sky in the Boston Public Garden. Fabrics used in the "Common" took their direction from the vibrant striped border fabric with its vining blue forget-me-knots and robust roses!

Cousins Eleanor Burns and Carol Selepec teamed up on this project! Eleanor speed pieced the top, and Carol brought life to the borders with her attractive machine quilted feathers.